AF269711

PRAISE FOR *THE COST OF WINNING*

"Dr. Gerald Gurney was a great man. He was a pleasure to work with when I was athletic director at the University of Oklahoma. His goal was to graduate every student-athlete. A man of great character and integrity."
—Steve Owens, 1969 Heisman Trophy winner; athletic director, University of Oklahoma, 1996–1997

"Each chapter in *The Cost of Winning* reminded me of what a privilege it was to learn from Gerry. His memoir critiques the commercialization of college sports and follows his journey as an advocate for exploited college athletes. This book is a must-read for anyone wanting to understand the true 'cost of winning.'"**—Richard M. Southall, EdD, professor, Department of Sport and Entertainment Management; director, College Sport Research Institute, University of South Carolina**

"In this poignant memoir, Gerald Gurney provides an insider's view of the challenges in supporting the academic goals of college athletes. He reveals how a multibillion-dollar industry promotes a narrative of academic success while undermining these athletes' chances to benefit from their promised educations. *The Cost of Winning* reflects Gurney's efforts to hold NCAA officials accountable."**—Ellen J. Staurowsky, EdD, professor of sports media, Ithaca College**

"In *The Cost of Winning*, Gerald Gurney offers an insightful look at the pitfalls of college sports and the struggles to course-correct. For anyone eager to understand the evolution of intercollegiate athletics, this book is for you."
—Andrew Zimbalist, PhD, professor emeritus of economics, Smith College; coauthor of *Unwinding Madness*

"Dr. Gerald Gurney was an outstanding leader in college athletics. He challenged us to think critically and focus on the welfare of student-athletes."
—Ursula Gurney, deputy athletics director, University of Missouri Kansas City; former president, National Association of Academics and Student-Athlete Development Professionals

"Gerald Gurney's *The Cost of Winning* gives a rare look at big-time college athletics from the academic perspective. This book is a testament to his devotion to supporting college students."—**Brian Davis, educational consultant and former athletic administrator, University of North Carolina and University of Texas; Gurney mentee and former Iowa State University student-athlete**

"*The Cost of Winning* explains why there is corruption in college sports: people cave. Faculty caves, administrators cave, presidents cave. Where most cave, Gerald Gurney stood tall. Color him Professor of Courage."—**Jon Ericson, founder of The Drake Group**

"As a friend and mentor, Dr. Gurney was the preeminent authority on collegiate athletics."—**Max Weitzenhoffer, faculty and former regent, University of Oklahoma**

"As a mentor and friend, Dr. Gurney's unwavering support helped me graduate and equipped me for life after athletics. His impact on my journey has been profound."—**Renaldo Works, former University of Oklahoma student-athlete and NFL athlete; National Football Foundation National Scholar-Athlete**

"When Bob Hitch became the athletic director of Southern Methodist University, I knew Gerry Gurney was the right choice. The full story of this pivotal time is revealed in *The Cost of Winning*. Anyone aspiring to a career in this field must read it."—**Lynn Lashbrook, EdD, president and founder, Sports Management Worldwide**

"There are no words to describe what Dr. Gurney meant to me. He supported me and gave me opportunities that changed my life. I would not be where I am today without him."—**Annette Bryntesson-Moran, assistant dean of students, University of Oklahoma College of Engineering; Gurney mentee and former University of Oklahoma student-athlete**

"Dr. Gerald Gurney represents everything that is right about collegiate athletics. He saw potential in me that I was unable to see in myself. My successes today are linked to the support I received from Dr. G."—**Carl Anthony Pendleton, police captain, City of Norman; former University of Oklahoma student-athlete**

THE COST OF WINNING

AN INSIDER'S PERSPECTIVE ON EXPLOITATION AND GREED IN COLLEGE SPORTS

GERALD S. GURNEY

ROWMAN & LITTLEFIELD
Lanham • Boulder • New York • London

Published by Rowman & Littlefield
An imprint of The Rowman & Littlefield Publishing Group, Inc.
4501 Forbes Boulevard, Suite 200, Lanham, Maryland 20706
www.rowman.com

86-90 Paul Street, London EC2A 4NE, United Kingdom

British Library Cataloguing in Publication Information Available

Library of Congress Cataloging-in-Publication Data

Names: Gurney, Gerald Sherman, author.
Title: The cost of winning : an insider's perspective on exploitation and greed in college sports / Gerald S. Gurney.
Description: Lanham, Maryland : Rowman & Littlefield, 2025. | Includes bibliographical references and index. | Summary: "The Cost of Winning offers a firsthand account, from an award-winning senior-level athletic administrator, of how college athletics has morphed into quasi-professional athletic leagues while exploiting the athletes, higher education, and taxpayers. It is an unapologetic depiction of the winners and losers of the games behind the games"—Provided by publisher.
Identifiers: LCCN 2024039620 (print) | LCCN 2024039621 (ebook) | ISBN 9798881801465 (cloth) | ISBN 9798881801472 (epub)
Subjects: LCSH: College sports—Corrupt practices—United States. | College sports—Economic aspects—United States.
Classification: LCC GV351 .G869 2025 (print) | LCC GV351 (ebook) | DDC 796.04/3—dc23/eng/20240917
LC record available at https://lccn.loc.gov/2024039620
LC ebook record available at https://lccn.loc.gov/2024039621

♾️™ The paper used in this publication meets the minimum requirements of American National Standard for Information Sciences—Permanence of Paper for Printed Library Materials, ANSI/NISO Z39.48-1992.

Gerald often said, "You do all you can for your kids, and then you do even more." This guiding principle was the foundation of his approach to family and the countless students and mentees he inspired throughout his life. Driven by immense generosity and an unwavering commitment to excellence, Gerald was dedicated to helping students reach their fullest potential. Though Gerald originally set out to write this memoir for his daughter, this book is ultimately a tribute to *all* of his "kids"—the many people he guided with his profound wisdom, encouragement, and steadfast support. Within these pages, you will find a testament to Gerald's boundless dedication and care for every individual he embraced as part of his extended family.

Gerald Gurney with students at the University of Oklahoma Max Weitzenhoffer Graduation Reception, 2009. *University of Oklahoma Athletics*

CONTENTS

FOREWORD

Donna A. Lopiano

If you avoid sad or scary movies because the purpose of entertainment in your life is to uplift and you yearn for positive disengagement, this book may not be for you. If you are a fan of college sports who enjoys football and March Madness as an escape from political, societal, or workplace dysfunction, this book may not be your cup of tea. However, if you wish for college sports to be as beneficial for the students who play as they are for the coaches and administrators making six- and seven-figure salaries, this book is for you. Likewise, if you are one of the many fans enthralled with the extraordinary athleticism and drama of exciting and well-played college athletic contests, this honest behind-the-scenes look at the college athlete experience will most certainly satisfy your curiosity. Gerald Gurney's real-life intersections with legendary college athletes and coaching giants make compelling narratives but, more importantly, this book highlights the experiences of the thousands of young athletes recruited by college coaches each year with promises of meaningful college degrees and slim chances—just 4 percent—of playing even one day in the NFL or NBA. This book offers a glimpse into their reality and may help you determine whether reform in collegiate athletics is a realistic expectation.

Gerald Gurney created the first sophisticated, research-supported collegiate academic support program that successfully addressed the academic unpreparedness and learning disabilities of talented college athletes. These athletes were specially admitted to academically demanding flagship universities without meeting the universities' usual academic admissions standards. Rather than taking the easier route of placing athletes in less challenging courses and majors—an approach still commonly used today to meet the NCAA's ridiculously low academic eligibility standards—Gurney, the educator, chose the more difficult path of remediation. Gurney reveals how the NCAA is complicit in academic fraud by manufacturing a graduation rate metric that deliberately obscures the failure of basketball and football players to graduate.

Gurney epitomized integrity amid an NCAA Division I culture in which telling the truth about rules violations committed by winning head coaches is treasonous and cause for demotion or termination. In this environment, sullying the glitter of the institution's brand is viewed as an act of disloyalty. He exposes the athletics seduction of college presidents, the symbiotic relationship between wealthy boosters and college coaches, and the involvement of a crooked state governor. Additionally, Gurney discusses athletic directors whose measures of success are ticket sales, fundraising, and big-money television contracts. He also explains the under-the-table "meat market" used to entice top players—regardless of their current college affiliations—with offers of cash, cars, and jobs for their parents. You also gain insight into the experience of attending an all-day NCAA infractions hearing and learn why the NCAA enforcement process is incredibly impotent.

It might surprise you to learn that the "dumb jock" stereotype is far from accurate. In fact, the vast majority of Division I men's basketball and football players who are specially admitted with learning disabilities and/or reading, writing, or math deficiencies actually have average or above-average IQs. It shouldn't surprise us that these talented athletes are more likely to come from lower socioeconomic backgrounds, under-resourced K–12 institutions, and educational environments where learning disabilities are much less likely to be diagnosed. Gerald Gurney was not surprised by this. He recognized the unrealized potential of these underprepared athletes, which, when coupled with what he described as their "dogged work ethic," enabled them to succeed academically by taking advantage of the academic support programs he created. However, Gurney's description of academic fraud at many NCAA Division I institutions is more troubling. He illustrates the academic struggles athletes face when they sense that those around them do not believe that they belong in higher education. This situation worsens when head coaches—who are often the most influential figures in these athletes' lives—fail to support them as students. Instead of motivating, encouraging, and ensuring that athletes apply their dogged work ethic in the classroom, these coaches appear too busy to act as educators or responsible mentors.

Gurney's experience, longevity, and gravitas made him one of very few rules compliance and academic support experts whose reputation and integrity could withstand opposition from powerful coaches and college presidents. He willingly donned the mantle of educational leadership as an outspoken critic of athlete academic exploitation. Few educators with his level of knowledge in research and academic support were able to rise to senior-level administrative positions encompassing both rules compliance and academic support. Even fewer were willing to risk everything to consistently and persistently speak truth to power.

Donna A. Lopiano, PhD, president of Sports Management Resources, past president of The Drake Group, and coauthor of Unwinding Madness: What Went Wrong with College Sports and How to Fix It.

PREFACE

Rachel M. Gurney

T*he Cost of Winning* is the memoir of Gerald S. Gurney, PhD (1951–2022), an award-winning senior-level athletic administrator, professor, and leading expert in ethics in intercollegiate athletics. Over his more than forty-year career, Gerald worked directly with athletes striving to achieve the dream of a meaningful college degree and a career in professional sports. His experiences transformed him from a "true believer" in the NCAA's educational values to a nationally renowned critic of the greed and exploitation pervasive in big-time college sports. Through a combination of rigorous investigation and compelling narrative, Gerald exposes how this flawed system prioritizes profit over athlete well-being and how the true cost of winning is often borne by those who can least afford it.

Gerald Gurney was instrumental in advocating for reforms that prioritized the needs and rights of athletes, pushing for policies that balanced competitive success with academic and personal development. His efforts led to significant changes in how institutions address athlete well-being, including improved academic support systems. Gerald's dedication was not limited to policy changes; he actively engaged with students and colleagues, offering guidance and support that extended beyond professional obligations. His commitment to mentoring the next generation of leaders in athletics created a ripple effect, shaping the future of the field and fostering a culture of integrity and ethical responsibility. Gerald's legacy is a testament to the impact that one person can have on an entire industry, and his unwavering pursuit of fairness and excellence continues to drive positive change in the realm of college sports.

Gerald's memoir is not just a recounting of personal experiences; it is a clarion call for accountability and reform in an industry that has strayed far from its educational roots. Through his candid reflections, readers gain a profound understanding of the systemic issues plaguing college athletics, from the skewed priorities that favor profit over principle to the ethical compromises that undermine American universities. His narrative is a powerful reminder that behind the glittering facade of college athletics lies a world rife with ethical contradictions.

This book serves as a valuable resource for anyone invested in the future of college sports. It challenges all of us—whether administrators, educators, policymakers, or fans—to confront the uncomfortable truths about the state of intercollegiate athletics and to advocate for meaningful change. By sharing his experiences and insights, Gerald not only exposes the flaws in the system but also offers a blueprint for how reform might be achieved. His dedication to improving the lives of athletes and upholding academic integrity resonates throughout the book, making it a crucial read for those who seek to understand and rectify these issues.

Gerald illuminates the transformation of college sports from a benign attraction and curiosity (amateur model) into a lucrative entertainment industry (quasi-professional leagues). Through this exploration, readers will understand the myriad ways in which this pursuit of profit has overshadowed the ideals of American higher education. By examining the mechanisms of this critical evolution, Gerald demonstrates how institutional priorities have shifted at the expense of athletes, higher education, and taxpayers.

Through this rare behind-the-scenes look at major college athletic programs, Gerald offers an honest, brave, and sometimes humorous chronicle of the highs and lows of big-time college sports. He provides firsthand accounts of historic events such as the Southern Methodist University death penalty, the aftermath of Len Bias's tragic death at the University of Maryland, and a national football championship at the University of Oklahoma. Gerald pulls back the curtain on a range of administrative blunders, revealing how institutions safeguard their investments in celebrity coaches and the culture of self-preservation among college sports leaders. He also uncovers the coaches' code of silence and the practice of sacrificing individuals to shield athletic programs from scrutiny.

Gerald provides sharp insights into how college presidents, athletic directors, and coaches ensure star athletes are admitted and eligible to play at any cost. With this, he reveals how athletics has become a vehicle for exploitation that advances the personal ambitions of those in positions of power. Gerald dismantles the myth of the magical winning coach and scrutinizes unsustainable financial practices. Through this lens, college presidents are seen as powerless cheerleaders, unwilling or unable to alter the trajectory of soaring coaching salaries and the athletic facilities arms race. Most importantly, Gerald vividly brings to life the struggles of underprepared and overburdened athletes ensnared in the harsh grind of college athletics. In doing so, he challenges readers to confront systemic flaws and calls for a reevaluation of the values driving intercollegiate athletics.

Gerald wrote this memoir between 2013 and 2016. Following his passing in 2022, Gerald's family and friends, dedicated to honoring his legacy, collaborated to publish his memoir posthumously. Gerald found immense joy in supporting and celebrating the achievements of his students and colleagues, and it is in this spirit that we bring his memoir to you. It is our hope that his reflections guide you along your journey with wisdom, grit, and humor. May his insights strengthen your efforts to advance the vital work of advocating for athlete well-being and academic integrity in intercollegiate athletics.

Royalties from this book support students through donations to the Dr. Gerald S. Gurney Retention Scholarship Fund at the University of Oklahoma. Contributions to this fund are essential for providing deserving students with the means necessary to achieve their academic goals toward a prosperous future. To further support this cause, please visit give.oufoundation.org/ DrGurney. Your generosity makes a meaningful difference.

Rachel M. Gurney, PhD, is the daughter of Gerald S. Gurney, PhD. Rachel is a social scientist and faculty associate at the University of Wisconsin–Madison.

ACKNOWLEDGMENTS

The publication of this book was made possible through the work and determination of Gerald's family—his daughter, Rachel Gurney, and his spouse, Debra Stuart—as well as his friends and colleagues. Their commitment and expertise were instrumental in bringing Gerald's memoir to the public following his passing in 2022. Much gratitude to Sanford Thatcher for his invaluable publishing expertise throughout this journey. Special thanks to Mary Willingham and Donna Lopiano for their insightful contributions to the epilogue and foreword and to Dave Ridpath for providing critical context with his notes and references. Our appreciation also goes to Terri Moyer for her meticulous work on photo captions and to everyone who graciously provided endorsements for this book. We are profoundly grateful to The Drake Group and its members—many of whom were dear friends of Gerald's—for their continued advocacy in promoting academic integrity and athlete well-being in intercollegiate athletics. Finally, we express our heartfelt thanks to Rowman & Littlefield and our editor, Christen Karniski, for her thoughtful guidance and support throughout the publication process.

ONE

ATHLETICS IS NO CAREER FOR A NICE JEWISH BOY

What makes my story worthy of reading is where I have been and when I was there. Quite accidentally, I managed to be amid some of the most turbulent times and places in college athletics history as a firsthand observer. It has been a remarkable journey of triumphs and disasters. Along the way, I met great mentors, faculty, administrators, colleagues, and athletes who challenged me and shaped my views on college athletics. I experienced the highs and lows of athletics and everything in between. I had the privilege of working alongside many dedicated academic support advisers and other professionals and assisting thousands of athletes through their academic and athletic journeys.

I grew up in Cleveland Heights, Ohio, the youngest son of Orthodox Jewish parents. My father, Milton, immigrated to the United States from Poland in 1939, just three months before the Nazis invaded. Milton Gurney was the last child in his family to leave. He had a second-grade education in a country that highly restricted what Jews could do. My paternal grandparents, Nissan and Sarah, refused to leave Poland and fell victim to the Holocaust. Like most Jewish men in Europe, my father learned a trade. He became skilled in tailoring. My mother, Molly, was the daughter of emigrants from Minsk, Russia. She was born in America and graduated high school in Cleveland, Ohio. My maternal grandfather, Isaac, was a proud US Marine and later drove trolleys and buses for the Cleveland Transit System. My maternal grandmother, Dorthea, was a traditional strong Jewish woman who ran the household and most aspects of family life.

In America, my father worked at his nephew's shoe store, Saltzman's Shoes, in inner-city Cleveland at East 55th and Woodland until he was able to purchase the store. To help the family, my brothers and I learned how to sell shoes. The store was in a rough, crime-ridden area where robberies occurred frequently. My job at the store was to stand at the door with a large pipe to deter thieves. Thankfully, I never had to use it. Protecting our family's livelihood was serious business.

My parents sacrificed a great deal to provide a college education for my brothers and me, and we were expected to succeed. Hard work was important and purposeful, and, for my parents, saving money for their children's futures meant the sacrifice of many standard luxuries common during the 1950s and 1960s. For example, our family didn't have a car until I was in high school. It was a new 1960 Chevy Bel Air, and my father was so proud that he would lay a blanket over the car's hood to put it to bed at night. Its successor, a 1970 Chevy Nova, received the same treatment.

Other than family celebrations like bar mitzvahs and weddings, I recall only one instance, when I was thirteen years old, in which my parents went on what might be called a "date." They took a taxi to Shaker Square to see the 1964 hit movie *My Fair Lady*, starring Rex Harrison and Audrey Hepburn. It was snowing heavily, and on the return trip, the taxi got into an accident. Although nobody was hurt, my parents were traumatized as if God had sent them a message. Never again would they attempt to venture out for entertainment.

My parents taught me that my brain would be far more valuable than my brawn and that education would ensure a fulfilling life in America. They were absolutely correct, and although I didn't always appreciate that lesson in my youth, I understand it now. Although my father knew absolutely nothing about athletics, he attended one of my night football games where I played both offensive and defensive tackle for the Cleveland Heights High Tigers. One-platoon football was still in vogue. It was a warm fall evening, and I remember cooling myself off with a cold, wet towel during a time-out. Suddenly, I heard my father's frantic voice in his Polish accent behind me. Seeing my head covered with a towel and worried that I was injured, my father rushed from the stands to check on me. This was a bit humiliating, but it was nice knowing my father cared. In hindsight, it was perfectly in character for my dad and a sweet gesture. That was the first and last time he attended a game during my athletic career, which included high school football, wrestling, and shot put, as well as one year of football at Heidelberg College in Tiffin, Ohio.

In my culture, only a few careers were considered acceptable: medicine, law, business, or scholarship (Talmudic or academic). The constant message from my parents to me and my brothers was that education was a ticket to a better life, and all other activities, such as athletics, were

Gerald Gurney with football team, Cleveland Heights High School, 1968

mere diversions from the serious pursuit of education. It was clear that my parents wanted a better life for their children. My eldest brother, Nelson, pursued a brilliant career in medicine. My middle brother, Sheldon, pursued business. I was the designated lawyer. After graduating cum laude with an undergraduate degree in English Education from The Ohio State University, I entered Ohio Northern University College of Law. I found the study of law to be tedious and trivial, and much to the dismay of my parents, I left after one semester and returned to Columbus to find a job and enroll in graduate school to pursue a career in higher education. My father was so utterly disappointed that he nearly sat shiva for me (a period of mourning observed by Jews). Until the day he died, my father never really understood why a Jew would pursue a livelihood in intercollegiate athletics.

After leaving law school, I took advantage of the free tuition benefit for employees and worked at Ohio State's veterinary college as a lab technician while enrolled in the graduate program for student personnel work in higher education. This job required me to clean up after animals housed in large laboratories each day. I arrived at work at 5:00 a.m. and—with my supervisor's permission—took a few hours off in the afternoon to attend classes. Often, I rushed to class wearing a smock covered with feces from various species and sat in the back to avoid offending my classmates. In one of those classes, I met a fellow graduate student who later became my wife, Debra Stuart.

In 1976, after a short engagement, Debra and I eloped and were married by a justice at Columbus City Hall. This joyous event was shortly followed by tragedy when we learned my mother had passed away. She was only fifty-nine.

After completing my master's in student personnel work in higher education, I began my first professional job as a residence hall director and academic adviser for students on probation at Grinnell College—a highly selective, small, private liberal arts college in Iowa. Debra and I shared a single contract for a total salary of $8,000 per year, plus room and board. In the small thriving town of Grinnell, Iowa, we actually saved money. In 1978 I started a doctoral program in higher education administration at Iowa State University. I worked as the university's tutoring coordinator for the entire student population and as a coun-selor for high-risk students from minority populations at the student counseling center. My dream job was to be an academic adviser and teach at a university.

My career in big-time college sports began unremarkably. I had not planned nor sought a career in college athletics administration, and I viewed college athletes as just another student group in higher educa-tion. I had no idea I was preparing for a lengthy career working with college athletes. Shortly after defending my dissertation and completing my doctorate, I discovered a job opening in academic advising at Iowa State University. What was to become a forty-six-year stint in big-time college sports—much of it at senior administrative levels in academics and compliance—was an unplanned journey through some of the most fascinating and terrifying moments in intercollegiate athletics.

IOWA STATE UNIVERSITY

"They Can't Read!"

owa State University was undergoing turnovers in football and men's basketball. Donnie Duncan—former assistant coach at the University of Oklahoma under the great Barry Switzer—had just finished his first season as head coach at Iowa State, and Johnny Orr was hired away from the University of Michigan to rejuvenate the Iowa State Cyclones' struggling basketball program.[1] Donnie Duncan would later return to Oklahoma to become its athletic director. In football, Iowa State perennially lost to its bitter in-state rival, the University of Iowa, and sat near the bottom of the Big 8, in which the universities of Oklahoma and Nebraska vied for trips to the Orange Bowl and national championships.

I was one of about 250 applicants called to interview in December 1979 for the position of athletic academic counselor with Athletic Director Lou McCullough, Associate Athletic Director Max Urick, and Head Football Coach Donnie Duncan. During my interview, I got the sense that all three of them felt nervous about the academic status of the athletes and needed answers to what they considered monumental problems. They sought a counselor to work directly with their revenue-sport athletes because they had no one to offer personal academic advice and survival skills. PhDs working with athletes on academic performance were a rarity, and I'm certain the department considered it a bonus they could use to recruit athletes. I was hired. The only other academic support professionals working in college athletics at the time were Drs. Ursula Walsh at Nebraska, Lynn Lashbrook at Missouri, and Ann Mayo at Ohio State.

I started in athletics at Iowa State in the spring of 1980, fresh out of my doctoral program. My salary was $15,500. Although this may seem low, practically everyone around me—including coaches—made a similar salary. We were all educators working for a nonprofit public university, after all. The rapidly escalating salaries of coaching staff and administrators came a few years later when the television broadcast of games became a vast new revenue stream for big-time football and basketball.

I vividly recall a locker room visit by President W. Robert Parks before a football game, with his greeting to me, "Keep them eligible, Gerry." Naively, I asked myself why the university's president was concerned about athletes' eligibility. I found the comment odd then but understood it better later in my career. I was enthralled with the crowds at the football and basketball games and the importance people placed on the outcome of the events. Feeling part of a team was exhilarating. Even the university's president knew what part I played and seemingly valued it. I believed in the NCAA hype that college football and basketball created opportunities for socioeconomically disadvantaged students and my work would benefit their futures. For athletes who did not graduate, I believed their time in college gave them exposure to people and ideas

Gerald Gurney at Iowa State University, 1980

they would not have otherwise received. At the time, I was convinced that college sports served the greater good.

My initiation into the world of intercollegiate athletics brought new colleagues and friends that would last a lifetime. My first call was from a young Prentice Gautt, the new assistant commissioner of the Big 8 Conference, welcoming me into the exciting world of intercollegiate athletics academic advisement. He was the first Black football player at the University of Oklahoma and a pioneer in integrating athletics at southern universities. He played football for the great Bud Wilkinson in the late 1950s, graduated, and went on to a career in the NFL. Later, he coached at Missouri while pursuing a doctorate in counseling psychology. While at Missouri, he took on the role of counseling and advising athletes. Prentice was a soft-spoken, thoughtful, gentle giant of a man whom I admired immensely, and thankfully he took me on as a mentee. He understood every aspect of the proper roles of athletics in higher education and was a rare voice of reason when athletics grew out of control. We remained great friends until his untimely death in 2005.

The profession of athletic academic counseling was at its genesis. The academic advising of athletes was typically done by coaches who took on the role as an aside to coaching football or basketball. Their primary objective was to keep their athletes eligible. Concepts of student development, learning skills, and career interests were foreign to them. I was on the ground floor of a burgeoning profession. It afforded me the opportunity to develop new approaches to strengthening the academic performance of this special student population. My research interests carried me into career development, what factors into athletes' choices of colleges, and primarily the academic performance and learning skills of college athletes. The success or failure of athletes at the university and loss of key athletes' eligibility would dramatically affect the fortunes of a team and futures of coaches and administrators. My role was foundational to the business of college athletics. Without this part, everything could be sent tumbling. This work was behind the scenes and, if done correctly, would not be noticed by the public. I oversaw thousands of variables for many athletes in many classes, my objective being that they meet graduation and eligibility requirements. If done successfully, the pieces of this large jigsaw puzzle would come together, and the games could go on as planned. I was well suited for the enormous responsibilities of overseeing students' well-being and the future of sports programs.

Being Jewish, I come from a long line of worriers. I recognized that even a slight oversight or an act of panic from an athlete could easily become a case of academic misconduct and result in loss of eligibility and my job. I relied on the integrity of a hundred or more tutors to remain within the limits of academic assistance without cheating. It was an awesome responsibility that kept me awake at night, drawing up alternative plans for the possibilities of any mishap. My instincts as a caretaker made me particularly adept as an academic support professional in athletics. I loved the responsibility and enjoyed spending time with my students.

Athletes and coaches were public figures but not yet the celebrities of today. At Iowa State, it was understood that most athletes were not there to pursue professional athletic careers, and coaches were not measured entirely by winning records. My wife entered her doctoral program in higher education at Iowa State, and we joined the coaching families of football and men's basketball. Several coaching assistants later became head coaches. Coach Duncan and basketball coach Orr truly appreciated my dedication to their athletes, and I felt supported when support was needed.

My first observation about my athletes was their extreme difficulty with reading and comprehending college textbooks. In the evenings, I conducted a supervised study with struggling freshmen and athletes in the residence hall dining facility. At times I asked them to read a passage from their textbooks to me, and it was obvious that some of them could not read at all. Many read too slowly to get through their assignments in a reasonable time. I feared most minority athletes from economically disadvantaged backgrounds could not compete in any class demanding rigorous study. The State of Iowa had an excellent educational system and often achieved the highest ACT scores in the nation. The university drew excellent students for its highly competitive engineering and agricultural programs. Iowa was sparsely populated, and without high numbers of talented NCAA Division I players, its football team recruited from urban areas in the region such as Chicago, Saint Louis, and Kansas City. This approach made for a wide disparity between the academic preparedness of the football and men's basketball athletes and the rest of the student body.

To further complicate matters, the NCAA's minimum initial-eligibility standards were at their weakest in history.[2] The 2.0 rule, as it was known, established in 1973, required athletes to earn a C average or 2.0 grade point average from high school to qualify for a scholarship and competition. This standard could include letter grades for physical education and other nonacademic coursework. In fact, one could graduate as a special education student and still qualify for an NCAA scholarship.[3]

Shortly after I started my first spring semester, I was tipped off by one of the football coaches that I was to receive a real challenge in the fall. Marcus (a pseudonym) arrived from the South Side of Chicago in August. An enormous defensive tackle, six feet six inches tall and 280 pounds, Marcus's speed and athletic ability struck fear in his teammates. He had not applied for admission to the university nor completed the necessary paperwork for housing and enrollment. Marcus could neither read his application for admission nor sign his name, but he had graduated with a 2.0 from high school in special education. When asked to designate a college major, Marcus eagerly blurted out "engineering," for he was fascinated with trains and looked forward to working as a train engineer. I advised him to begin as an undecided major. While working with Marcus, I often heard reports from his instructors that he was falling asleep in classes. Donnie Duncan and Marcus's position coach noticed that Marcus would often doze off and snore during team meetings. After consulting with the medical staff, Marcus was referred to a physician, who diagnosed him with a form of narcolepsy and prescribed a stimulant designed to keep him attentive. Marcus eventually stopped taking the prescription because it disturbed his ability to sleep in class.

Although Marcus was an extreme example of athletes admitted to academically competitive institutions for their athletic abilities without regard for their preparedness for the classroom, I noticed that several other football and men's basketball players also had severe challenges reading. They had excelled in athletics because of their innate abilities and the rote learning methods in football and basketball. Learning the playbook was accomplished by repeating plays hundreds or thousands of times.

Another clue about the depth of athletes' academic challenges came from a defensive end named "Billy." I summoned Billy to my office to inform him that he needed to plan for summer school enrollment due to his poor academic performance. He then proceeded to inform me he could not attend summer school because, as he put it, "I need to make me some money! You know, M-U-N-Y!"

As any practicing professional would, I set out to analyze the scope of the problem I was facing in order to devise an effective remediation plan. I hired a reading specialist from the university who administered the Nelson-Denny Reading Test to all football and men's basketball players. We found that about 10 percent of the teams were reading below the fourth-grade level, and nearly all were reading well below the ninth-grade level (the level at which basic college textbooks are written). Armed with this information, I developed an aggressive required reading program for my athletes, including remedial reading training with a certified reading specialist. This was in addition to an in-season schedule that included the equivalent of full-time devotion to athletics and their studies. I learned later that this program was groundbreaking—unheard of in college athletics. Academic support programs such as mine didn't resemble the mega-million-dollar programs of today, housed in opulent dedicated academic centers. For Iowa State, it meant Brian Davis, a graduate assistant, and I working days advising students and nights monitoring the tutoring and reading development programs. We were young and idealistic.

Although only about twenty-four full-time academic professionals were working with college athletes around the country at the time, what was novel about the Iowa State program was that, upon arrival, athletes were assessed for academic preparedness and career interest. An attempt was made for remediation and to provide college major advisement based on personality and career interests. This was the first assessment program in the nation for college athletes, which would later become the standard for programs nationwide.

At Iowa State, reading remediation of college athletes offered mixed results. For those athletes who embraced the assistance, I saw rapid progress. Others resisted the assistance and opted for the courses of least resistance, taking classes with little challenge and no foreseeable personal benefit except athletic eligibility. The standard for maintaining eligibility was merely passing twenty-four semester credit hours from any curriculum. Many improved their skill levels and were able to earn their diplomas. Others maintained their eligibility and left Iowa State with the memory of competing at a high level at a great university. Marcus survived his freshman year, earned his eligibility, got into an argument with his position coach early in his sophomore year, and took a bus back to Chicago.

With my first assistant, former track athlete and graduate student Brian Davis, I carved out an effective and modern academic support system that operated on a very limited budget. Brian and I worked together in a closet-sized office (converted from a vending machine room) in the Olsen Building. Brian and I didn't know enough to complain. We did the best we could with the limited resources available. Brian went on to advise at the University of North Carolina at Chapel Hill, then the University of Texas, where he directed the academic support program for Longhorns football. Brian is one of the fortunate academic support professionals who survived for years with his integrity and sanity intact.

I developed profound respect for the athletes who lacked academic skills yet committed to improvement. They embraced difficult tasks and the common goal of devotion to their teammates. This personal discipline served them well into the future. College athletes also compensate for academic weaknesses with communication skills and social charm. They tend to be likable, so people would want to help them. Some athletes become local celebrities and garner a following of instructors, friends, acquaintances, and romantic interests eager to help them academically.

Soon after I arrived at Iowa State in 1980, a notable junior college transfer athlete phenom arrived who offered new hope for Cyclones football. Charles (a pseudonym) was a large, fast, and tough running back who ran over opponents and thrilled Iowa State fans. Although he had an engaging personality, Charles's ambition was to go pro, and he made it clear that he was not interested in going to class or doing anything to disturb his sleep other than football. In the spring of 1980, Charles had hardly gone to class, and his eligibility was doubtful. The Big 8 Conference first-team running back was in serious jeopardy of being academically ineligible for the following fall season. Time was running out. Amazingly, there remained enough outstanding work and exams for him to salvage his semester. I invited him to spend an all-nighter with me the weekend before exams to write his papers and study. I felt the weight of Iowa State fans everywhere and the football coaches to create a miracle. Thanks to Charles's effort and my organizational skills, Charles earned his eligibility and I became known as an official miracle worker. When a football or basketball season completed, I felt I was handed the fate of their programs. It was up to me to bring an out-of-control airplane in for an emergency landing. It was a power rush.

I learned later that my time at Iowa State was still an age of innocence in intercollegiate athletics. The stakes for winning were not as high as at other schools, and Iowa State seemed to have big-time sports in perspective. The NCAA limited television broadcasts, and huge revenues realized from the 1984 *NCAA v. Board of Regents* lawsuit were not yet infused into athletics departments.[4] The NCAA's vision of amateurism existed for a brief time, when there was truly an offseason for athletes, when offseason strength and conditioning workouts were actually voluntary, and when athletes worked summer jobs. It was typical for assistant coaches to teach at the university. Usually, coaches taught physical education courses such as Theories of Football, Racquetball, Wrestling, or other elective courses for students. This was a remnant of the role of coaches as educators in big-time college sports. I had the sense that in the early 1980s—at the less competitive Division I programs such as Iowa State and with the coaches on staff—I was a member of a larger team, and everyone was focused on the well-being of athletes and the university. There remained a concept of contributing to the university's mission and teaching athletes life lessons. At that time athletes could take advantage of offseason opportunities offered by the university to learn and grow. That was soon to change.

Donnie Duncan had some success with his football teams in the early 1980s, including three successive wins over in-state rival University of Iowa and some of Hayden Fry's great teams, as well as a tied score against a great Oklahoma team in Norman. Yet Donnie suddenly resigned after the 1983 season. Members of his coaching staff went on to take head coaching positions in other programs—Mack Brown at the University of North Carolina and University of Texas, Sparky Woods at South Carolina and Virginia Military Institute, and Jim Williams at Simpson College—all of whom remained close friends of mine throughout my career. Abruptly, coaches and their spouses (whom I also regarded as close friends) were gone collectively overnight. I had not anticipated the sudden abandonment following turnover of the

Gerald Gurney and Donnie Duncan, 1993

football program, and loss of the coaches I had befriended affected me deeply. I enjoyed my close relationships with the entire staff. We were a family, and I had not yet learned that the regular departure and arrival of coaches was common. The sudden departure of coaches hardened me for what would become routine in my future. Although my position was secure as part of the department's administration, I felt the profound loss of the staff I had started with and learned from. Donnie Duncan would remain a close friend and mentor, and our paths would cross again in the future.

Following Duncan's departure from Iowa State, Athletic Director Max Urick hired Jim Criner from Boise State to head coach Iowa's football team. With much fanfare, the banner draped as the backdrop of his press conference read, "Things Are Finer with Criner." Criner would be the coach who introduced me to widespread, blatant cheating in college athletics and my first experience with a coach who appeared to have no connection with the university. During what was to be one season at Iowa State with Criner, we clashed on more than one occasion.

In 1983, college presidents began to exert their authority over college athletics. They were embarrassed by academic scandals such as the 1982 University of Georgia scandal involving pressure placed on English instructor Jan Kemp to submit passing grades. I was deeply influenced by the 1982 case of Kevin Ross, a basketball player at Creighton University who, after four years of playing, left without having learned how to read. The front page of the *Omaha World-Herald* showed Kevin in a class of elementary schoolchildren in Kansas City taking reading lessons. The story was a disgrace for Creighton, higher education, and college athletics. There was something terribly wrong with how Kevin was admitted as an NCAA qualifier without the necessary skills to compete in the classroom, how he maintained his eligibility through four years of competition, and how the university failed to educate him—exploiting his athletic talent.[5] It seemed to me that this constituted the worst form of abuse. It led me to conclude that there was an institutional responsibility to be more than just *eligibility brokers*. Universities need to actually educate their athletes. I felt a deep commitment to this philosophy and believed what I created at Iowa State was on the right course. Unfortunately, the responsibility to provide a real education to athletes did not seem to be a goal for most university athletics programs. The singular task of maintaining eligibility was their goal.

In April 1983, Max Urick asked me to meet with the Athletics Council (an oversight committee of faculty, students, and alumni) to discuss my assessment and reading improvement programs for the football and men's basketball programs. He was proud of my program and thought the faculty would be interested since it would benefit their relations with the university. My presentation included details of the assessments used, findings, and the remedial reading program. It was well received by the council. The following day I received a flood of calls from media sources around the world, including the *London Times*, the *Los Angeles Times*, the *New York Times*, *Sports Illustrated*, and more. A reporter in the room picked up my comments related to the reading readiness of our athletes. During my presentation, I mentioned that 95 percent of football and men's basketball players read below the ninth-grade level, and 10 percent read below the fourth-grade level and could be considered functionally illiterate. Unwittingly, I confirmed what many in the public believed: some woefully underprepared athletes were admitted to competitive universities solely for their athletic

Kevin Ross sued Creighton University under a theory of educational malpractice and breach of contract for exploiting him for his basketball skills without affording him the academic support he needed to be successful as a student and the time he needed to take full advantage of those services.[a] At the time his athletic eligibility expired, Ross had a seventh-grade reading level and was thirty-two credits short of the number he needed to graduate. Although the court found that Ross had a cause of action under breach of contract, it was determined that Ross could not recover compensation under educational malpractice because such a determination would create the likelihood that other students dissatisfied with their grades and educational experiences might seek similar relief.[b]

talents. Although the statement accurately described the problem from a clinical perspective, I touched on certain sensitivities that the football program did not wish to share with the world. The story suddenly cast a spotlight on me, and I developed a reputation as a builder and innovator. Although Johnny Orr had no issue with what I had said and thought of it as old news, Jim Criner screamed that my statements had forever ruined his recruiting.

Criner permitted a player who was a nonqualifier to practice and play. Throughout a two-year-long NCAA investigation, Criner claimed he had no knowledge of it. I furnished a memo reminding Criner of his ineligibility, which I also copied to the athletic director. This violation was an example of one in a long list of allegations. In 1986, the president of Iowa State, Gordon Eaton, fired Criner, but many believed that Criner was sacrificed as a means to relax NCAA penalties. Whether Eaton sacrificed Criner for the university's good or not is inconsequential. Eaton did Iowa State University and college athletics a great service. Criner never returned to college coaching.

What I learned from Criner was the principle of plausible deniability. Staff understood that protecting the head coach from allegations was the ultimate objective and falling on one's sword for the program's good was essential. The unwritten penalty for pointing a finger at the head coach was banishment from moving up in the profession. The college coaching profession is a close fraternity with a secretive pledging system. Those starting college coaching begin as graduate assistants. The loyalty of aspiring graduate assistant coaches is often tested by performing minor inducements for recruits or extra benefits for players, like providing transportation for players, equipment and apparel to recruits, or even small amounts of cash for essentials.

What I accomplished at Iowa State was the establishment of what is considered the first college program in the nation to assess and address academic problems associated with athletes. Supporting athletes who had difficulty with reading, or who could not read, was and is the correct approach to institutional responsibility. It attacks a real problem that coaches, athletic administrators, and NCAA staff have often chosen to ignore. Those in the business of athletics like to say, "Just keep them eligible." However, the unpreparedness of college athletes, particularly in men's basketball and football, remains. College athletics tend to mask this problem with a barrage of promises of academic reform.

The prospect of leaving Iowa State was a difficult decision for me. It was a somewhat comfortable place for Debra and me, and we considered Ames our home. The people of Iowa were extraordinarily welcoming and seemed to place big-time sports in proper perspective.

THREE

SOUTHERN METHODIST UNIVERSITY

Pickpockets at the Gallows

Following a screaming match with Jim Criner at Iowa State, I began looking at other career opportunities. My wife had finished her doctoral program in higher education institutional research, and it seemed like a good time to explore other possibilities in athletics where my talents might be better appreciated. It was then that I heard of an assistant athletic director opening at football powerhouse Southern Methodist University (SMU). Petrina Long, the assistant athletic director for academic affairs at SMU, had taken a position in athletic administration at Columbia University.

In Texas during the early 1980s, money flowed from the oil boom. The Southwest Conference was the home of Texas football, and the personal identity of wealthy alumni rested on helping their schools win games. Dallas was a growing city with optimism everywhere. Debra was pregnant with our daughter, and we felt we were starting our lives and careers in a refreshingly cosmopolitan city. The theme song of the enormously popular TV series *Dallas* intoxicatingly ran through my mind as I drove past modern buildings that resembled shiny bars of gold.

As I prepared for my interview with Athletic Director Bob Hitch, I realized this was serious college athletics. SMU was consistently in the conversation for national championships. "Mustang Mania" (a concept created by former SMU Athletic Director Russ Potts) was running at a fever pitch. Just before I was to interview in June 1984, news broke that the NCAA was wrapping up an investigation of recruiting inducements and extra benefits at SMU, and its Committee on Infractions would soon levy penalties against the school.[1]

I interviewed with Hitch at a local restaurant. He seemed like a strong, unflappable, and highly capable athletic administrator. Apart from the circumstances surrounding the pay-for-play scandals at SMU, Hitch was one of the best administrators with whom I worked in athletics. At lunch, I asked Hitch if there was anything I needed to know about the investigation and allegations of extra benefits and inducement to SMU football players. He stated that the university would go on probation for a couple of years and that all matters pertaining to the allegations had been cleaned up. I was told the program was set to move forward, and this probation would be just a mere bump in the road. This was only partially true. Later, I learned that payments to new recruits had stopped but continued for returning football athletes. SMU was a great university, Hitch sounded optimistic, and the thrill associated with a top football program in an exciting city lured me into accepting the position.

Living in Texas demonstrated the importance of football and winning games. The university is located next to Highland Park, an island of extreme wealth in the city. The high school sported an athletic complex as nice as many college stadiums. The university used Texas Stadium, home of the Dallas Cowboys, to play its home games. Dave Bliss was the head men's basketball coach, and Bobby Collins was the head football coach. My offices were housed in the football complex next to the coaching offices in Ownby Stadium. The remainder of the administrative and coaching offices were located in Moody Coliseum. The priority of my role—to maintain the academic eligibility of football athletes—was obvious. To entertain faculty, I was assigned a thirty-seat suite at home games, where liquor was served with catered fine dining. The implication was that well-fed and entertained faculty would be lenient on football players.

My wife, Debra, was pregnant at this time and worked as assistant to the provost of the university. Shortly before we were to leave for the Aloha Bowl in Hawaii, our team's reward for becoming co-champions of the Southwest Conference, our daughter Rachel was born—a joyous occasion that gave us just as much reason to celebrate.

A wealthy alumnus, Jack Ryan, was implicated in providing extra benefits and felt he needed to make amends by building a state-of-the-art academic facility for SMU athletes. The only clue I could observe regarding the extra benefits athletes were receiving was in the SMU parking lot reserved for football players, which was in front of my office. When the football players arrived for practice in the afternoons, the lot was filled with late-model sports cars such as BMWs and the popular Pontiac Firebirds—a stark contrast to my 1980 Plymouth Horizon.

My first experience working at a university that had recently undergone an investigation and was found in violation of major infractions was valuable and insightful. It heightened my awareness of the NCAA rules manual outside of academic legislation and the pressures brought to bear on athletics programs under such scrutiny. My attitude toward athletics had also begun to evolve from being a true believer in intercollegiate athletics' contributions to higher education and the character development of student-athletes, to critically questioning the value of big-time sports in academe.

Lonnie Kliever, one of the most highly respected faculty members at SMU at the time, helped to sharpen my focus and attitudes regarding college athletics. Kliever, an ethics professor at SMU's Perkins School of Theology and chair of the Department of Religious Studies, was the faculty athletics representative for the university. A faculty athletics representative (FAR) is appointed by the president to represent the institution at conventions, certify student-athlete eligibility, and preside over governance of the program.[2] We shared many discussions of important issues regarding the special admissions process of athletes to competitive universities, the value of competitive athletics at universities, and whether intercollegiate athletics builds character or merely reflects character. He was the finest FAR I have worked with and an outstanding servant of the university. Kliever was also the chief institutional investigator for violations that led up to the death penalty applied to SMU. He was widely known for his integrity and was credited for his investigation of the scandal. Born in Corn, Oklahoma, Kliever suffered from rickets as a child, and it stunted his growth and the formation of the bones in his legs. Physically, Professor Kliever stood less than five feet tall. Intellectually he was a giant who taught me about the value of perseverance.

While at SMU, I had the pleasure of working with truly outstanding staff. Among them was the finest sports information director I've ever known, Larry White, who maintained professionalism through the darkest days of SMU athletics history. He went on to finish his brilliant career at the University of Alabama. Barbara Camp, the senior women's administrator for athletics, was my supervisor and a voice of reason. She continued her career in athletics administration at Auburn University. Doug Smith was an outstanding fundraiser with whom I would work later at Oklahoma. Dudley Parker, who took over as the interim athletic director after the death penalty, also taught me a great deal. Parker's sage advice about compliance: "If something smells bad, it's probably a violation."

SMU was a fine liberal arts institution that insisted upon rigorous academic standards for all its students. There were no easy majors or lenient "jock docs" who would assign unearned grades. The athletics program maintained a high graduation rate, and I took great pride in scholar-athletes and academic achievement awards earned by my students. During my time at SMU, for three consecutive years, the National Football Foundation honored us with the Scholar-Athlete Award, which goes to the nation's top academic achievers in college football. One of my favorite scholars was Clark Hunt. He was the son of oilman Lamar Hunt, who later passed his ownership of the Kansas City Chiefs to his son. Clark was an exceptional student and soccer player who was destined for greatness.

Faculty attitudes toward SMU's athletics program became increasingly hostile after the 1984 NCAA probation. This worsened after imposition of the 1987 death penalty. Many faculty regarded the program as quasi-professional, which brought great shame upon the university and, more importantly, their academic reputations. Yet at no time did I sense that individual faculty members acted on their anger by retaliating against the athletes.

College presidents are seduced by the public platform enabled by Division I athletics programs. A champion football or basketball team can mean opportunities to get their campus into the national consciousness.[3] Often college presidents are mere pawns of influential donors who live vicariously through the fortunes of a winning football team.[4] Such appeared to be the case at SMU. Donors compare the success of football teams as they would any business venture. They hire the best coaches at any cost, buy the best labor through legal and illegal means, and build the finest facilities. Particularly in our country's Southeast and Southwest regions, the importance of winning in football is embedded in the psyche of boosters. Losses are taken so personally that they require immediate action, and winning programs reflect boosters' personal successes. At SMU, a loss to the University of Texas would mean the necessity for boosters to buy the finest running back or whatever position was needed. Boosters would work with football assistant coaches to identify specific targets for the team.[5]

This symbiotic relationship between boosters and coaches was openly practiced throughout the South. At SMU, there appeared to be competition for prized recruits among individual wealthy alums. Boosters would compete against one another for the privilege of bagging the services of talented athletes. It was recruiting gone wild, but SMU was not alone. I witnessed it firsthand in the football offices at SMU but also outside of my office during the post-death-penalty recruiting circus, when fifty-three players transferred to other institutions over a two-week period. It was an open meat market that occurred right under the NCAA's nose.[6]

My time at SMU lasted about three and a half years. It started with NCAA probation and ended a few months after the death penalty. It was my baptism in big-time sports, big-time football, and Texas football in particular. I felt betrayed by Bob Hitch, whom I had respected. He had hidden the fact that SMU's payments to players had continued. Hitch managed to convince the board of governors and its chair, Bill Clements, to end the practice of paying new recruits after 1983, but the veteran players continued to be paid. This was a secret Hitch hid very well. Hitch sacrificed the reputation of the university, its athletics program, and the professional reputations of his staff for a secretive agenda that exposed everyone.

In June 1986, the slush fund scandal erupted when a former football player, David Stanley, dismissed from the team due to drug use, appeared on television accusing SMU of continuing to pay him monthly after the 1984 NCAA probation. This demonstrated a wanton disregard for compliance with NCAA rules and was the fifth instance of major infractions committed by SMU since 1974. The university was now begging for the NCAA's harshest disciplinary measure—enactment of the newly legislated repeat offender's rule known as the "death penalty." SMU has the distinction of being the only university to have the death penalty levied against its football program by the NCAA. The athletics department was rapidly decimated, with coaches resigning and administrators leaving as quickly as possible. Everyone expected that radical changes were in SMU's future. In 1986, a faculty petition was distributed calling for an end to big-time sports at SMU.

In the final analysis, the course of SMU athletics was determined by the political strategy of the former Texas governor, Bill Clements, who was running for reelection. He chose to continue the payments to players because he feared reprisals from those disgruntled who might have gone public and the effect the scandal would have on voters.[7] For Governor Clements, this was a gamble that paid off. He won reelection. For the university, however, the scandal was a disaster that marred its reputation and stymied its athletics program for several decades. Sadly, these consequences resulted from greed and lack of leadership by those entrusted with fiduciary responsibility for the university.

After the death penalty, Bob Hitch and SMU president Donald Shields were paid a sum of cash and resigned from their positions. Shortly thereafter, Head Football Coach Bobby Collins resigned along with his staff. More than half of the athletics department staff resigned within months of the death penalty decision. Most were coaches and staff associated with the canceled football program, but administrators unrelated to the scandal left as well.

Although much has been written about the facts uncovered leading up to the death penalty and how it affected the campus, little is known about the onslaught of schools rushing to scavenge the remaining SMU players. The NCAA had banned competition for the 1987 season, and there was talk of canceling the 1988 season, as well, in recognition that developing a new football program takes time. The university had fifty-three players with remaining eligibility, and NCAA rules permitted athletes to transfer when their school was levied probation. I was assigned the unenviable task of transferring players who wished to complete their football eligibility elsewhere. SMU offered full scholarships to football players who wished to remain at the university, but few scholarship players took advantage of the offer.

I sat atop Ownby Stadium in my office at our new academic center, learning the transfer eligibility rules of athletic conferences around the nation, and advised my former players about the academic status of each school and conference they were considering. I worked with assistant coach recruiters across the country to help carefully place each athlete in a different school and curriculum. Below my office, in the stadium parking lot, athletes congregated to hear the pitches of nearly one hundred recruiters who were looking to pick up much-needed experience and athletic talent. Several of my athletes, without being prompted, unexpectedly wanted to share their recruiting experiences prior to arriving at SMU and what was being offered below at the Ownby parking lot meat market.

I offer this adage regarding whether the death penalty is an effective deterrent: Around 1800, more than two hundred crimes were punishable by hanging, including pickpocketing. As the condemned were to be hanged, huge crowds would gather—their attention fixed on the gallows. It was then and there that the crowd would be pickpocketed. The cheating that took place, as universities vied to gain the talents of SMU's former players, demonstrated that zealous athletics programs largely ignored the threat of the death penalty and the NCAA failed to uniformly enforce its rules.[8]

The athletes consistently stated that every school in the Southwest Conference, with the exception of Rice University, offered players cash and other inducements. The larger programs offered the most cash, but wealthy alumni from other schools participated as well. The scale of cheating in the Southwest Conference was larger than I imagined. SMU's cheating was not the most widespread; they just weren't able to cheat quietly. Division-I-caliber high school athletes in Texas expected to receive cash, cars, jobs for their parents, and other items of value to get their attention. Schools needed to participate in the bidding to be part of the game. It was the Texas way.[9]

In Dallas and around the nation, where the SMU players chose to transfer was big news. The players scattered into larger and smaller programs. What I found most amusing was that flagrant cheating and purchasing of players occurred right under the NCAA's nose yet was ignored. A player of mine was recruited by a Southeastern conference school in exchange for a new car titled to his grandmother. The players found the process quite amusing and I found the hypocrisy hilarious. The NCAA's Repeat Offender Rule, also known as the death penalty, would never be fully exercised against a Division I football program again. Although many other institutions were eligible for the death penalty, the NCAA understood that penalizing schools in this way damaged institutions too severely.[10]

The academic standards for incoming athletes changed significantly in 1986. A new approach entitled Proposition 48 passed due to academic scandals and embarrassments such as cases like Kevin Ross at Creighton and Jan Kemp at Georgia.[11] College presidents reacted to media exposure of athletes who could not read or write. The public was rapidly losing confidence in the NCAA's ability to establish academic standards for athletes and control widespread corruption. Proposition 48 (formally called NCAA Bylaw 5-1-(j)) was passed in 1983. The new rule abandoned the 2.0 grade point average requirement and established minimum standardized test scores and a core curriculum of college preparatory courses.[12] The effect of Proposition 48 improved the preparedness of athletes. Though fraud continued to occur via cheating on standardized tests and high school grade inflation, the rule made functional illiteracy a rarity.[13]

A. Kenneth Pye was hired from Duke to be SMU's president and restore integrity in its athletics program. Pye hired Doug Single from Northwestern to be SMU's athletic director. After the death penalty, the department's staff declined from about seventy-five to thirty-five. Shock of the rapid departure of the administration caused me great shame and embarrassment, including a return of the overwhelming feeling of abandonment.

Professor Kliever and I shared a feeling of profound betrayal by people whom we respected. Kliever was criticized on campus for being duped into believing Bob Hitch's claims that the program had been cleansed. I faced an uncertain future of what our program would become, amid the faculty upheaval and calls for reform on campus. After transferring the players with remaining eligibility in the spring of 1987, I explored my options in academic support at other athletics programs.

Initially, the cloud of working at SMU over my professional reputation and marketability concerned me. However, potential employers understood that what occurred at SMU had nothing to do with academic life. Professor Kliever went out of his way to describe my work as part of the solution rather than the problem. I brought a modern academic support program to campus and improved its integrity with the faculty.

While SMU dealt with the aftermath of the death penalty, the University of Maryland was reeling from the tragedy of Len Bias's untimely death. Working in athletics programs marred with challenges became my specialty. Although I had no way of knowing SMU's long-term devastation from the death penalty, I had a strong intuition that many years would pass before the university would recover from the scandal and heal itself. A major purge of the athletics program and university administration had occurred, and it was best for me to explore positions at other institutions.

FOUR

UNIVERSITY OF MARYLAND

Haunted by the Ghost of Len Bias

In the summer of 1987, I accepted a position as associate athletic director for academic support and compliance at the University of Maryland, College Park. Maryland was a great public university and original member of the Atlantic Coast Conference (ACC), primarily known for outstanding academic institutions and basketball with perennial powers such as North Carolina, Duke, Virginia, and North Carolina State. The move represented a radical change in my career, offering me a more diverse experience and an expansion of my duties from academics into compliance.

Being an associate athletic director for academics and compliance required me to straddle two complex roles: one advocating for athletes while safeguarding academic integrity and the other monitoring the rules compliance of coaches and administrators in internal affairs. This contradiction of roles and responsibilities made it very difficult for me to succeed with integrity. Monitoring academics is certainly challenging enough.

A constant friend and helpful confidant in my role as compliance officer was David Thompson, the ACC's associate commissioner for compliance. Thompson, a former NCAA enforcement staff member, was invaluable in helping me put violations in perspective and in safeguarding me from the pressures of my role as an institutional compliance officer. He often gave me the strength to carry on in this capacity rather than drop compliance altogether.

I handled both compliance and academic responsibilities while tending to the needs of more than five hundred athletes. Some coaches would not confide in me out of fear of being turned in for breaking the rules, and I would not compromise on rules compliance. In retrospect, it was clear that I did not have the resources to handle both of these roles, nor was it wise to handle such conflicting objectives. As a compliance director, I learned that coaches would not fully disclose the facts when asking for rule interpretations. The compliance responsibility gave me an unfettered view of athletics. Maryland served to confirm my doubts about the endemic corruption in college sports.

The University of Maryland had undergone a period of introspection following the death of its superstar first-team all-American basketball player, who had died while celebrating two nights after being drafted in the first round of the NBA by the Boston Celtics. Len Bias was a beloved local hero, and his use of cocaine and untimely death on June 19, 1986, shocked the entire campus and Washington, DC, area. Len had died of arrhythmia from a cocaine overdose. The wasted life of a celebrated athlete stirred many questions about the athletics department that the campus needed to resolve. How widespread was drug use among the athletes? Were the coaches aware of the drug use? What was the academic performance of Maryland's athletes? Were the athletes prepared when admitted to the university?[1]

John Slaughter, Maryland's chancellor, demanded an investigation of the athletics department and appointed two committees. One focused on drug use and the other on academic performance. In the aftermath of Len Bias's death, Maryland's very popular men's basketball coach Lefty Driesell was reassigned as a fundraiser for the Terrapin Club (the athletics department's fundraising organization). Robert Dull resigned as athletic director, and Maryland's program underwent further changes. J. Robert (Bob) Dorfman, a physicist and dean for the College of Computer, Mathematical, and Natural Sciences, was a much-respected faculty member on campus and was asked to lead the investigation. After nearly a yearlong investigation, the chancellor approved Dorfman's report recommendations.[2] Bob Dorfman was the chairperson of the search committee that hired me. He later told me that my campus interview positively impacted faculty and administrators at Maryland, and his discussion with Lonnie Kliever assured him that I had nothing to do with the problems SMU had experienced. Rather, my work had contributed to solutions.

After Len Bias's death, Driesell was replaced by legendary DC-area high school basketball coach Bob Wade. Driesell later went on to finish his coaching career at James Madison University. The University of Maryland conducted two internal reviews, including one by Acting Dean Dorfman and a former US attorney general that recommended changes to athletics department policy including stricter admission processes, enhancement of its new mandatory, random drug-testing program for athletes, higher academic minimums for athletes to remain eligible to play, and expanded tutorial and guidance staff (which Gerald Gurney played a major part in overhauling).

The University of Maryland afforded me the opportunity as an affiliate professor to teach graduate students pursuing their master's in sports management. Intercollegiate athletics was becoming increasingly intertwined with higher education, and its role as a revenue center in a nonprofit organization fascinated me. Teaching was a wonderful diversion from my role in the athletics department. I felt comfortable in the classroom and loved injecting humor into my lectures. Big-time college sport offers so many ironies that it is ripe for comedy. Academic freedom also permitted me to speak honestly about my observations. Teaching in the college classroom is a skill I improved over the years and expanded considerably—teaching the subjects of college athletics, ethical issues in college sports, and college academic reform. My students appreciated the conviction I infused into my lectures. The teaching process was rewarding for me, and I hope my students found it rewarding as well.

Lew Perkins, a former basketball player from Iowa who directed the Wichita State program, was hired in 1987 to direct Maryland's athletics program, replacing Richard Dull. Although I was primarily hired to run the academic support program, Perkins wanted me to handle the compliance responsibilities. He found my experience at SMU helpful, but I'm certain he wanted me to work on compliance because none of his senior administrators were interested in the job. Compliance was considered a no-win headache.

Bob Dorfman chaired the committee on academic integrity in athletics that reported the need for major changes at the University of Maryland in the special admissions of athletes and procedures regarding how they would be admitted. He also recommended that the university establish a modern academic support program for its athletes, one that included drug education. As a result, Maryland developed aggressive drug testing and drug education programs, which would serve as a national model.

Dorfman and I became close friends. He became my mentor and helped shape my views on athletic reform. In chairing the search committee for my position, I suspect that Dorfman sought an academic support professional who was tough enough to maintain integrity and able to withstand pressures from coaches. Certainly, surviving SMU during arguably the worst moment in college sports proved my ability to maintain integrity in the face of overwhelming pressure. The experience provided hard-learned lessons in compliance and the lengths boosters would go to in order to satisfy their egos. Cheating had infested higher education, and the stakes at SMU were higher than I ever imagined. I also suspected widespread corruption in college sports based on the meat market recruitment episode that occurred in SMU's parking lot. I would test the extent of college sports integrity when I moved to Maryland, a school and a conference known for its prestigious institutions and athletics programs.

The media markets covering Maryland athletics differed from Iowa State and SMU. The *Des Moines Register* covered Iowa State. The *Dallas Morning News* and the *Fort Worth Star* covered SMU. The *Washington Post* and the *Baltimore Sun* covered Maryland. Mark Asher of the *Washington Post* covered the Len Bias story and, for many years, continued writing stories about Maryland. He was an excellent and dogged investigative reporter who researched and delved deeply into his assignments. Even a casual observer would notice the difference in his journalistic talents.

After the death of Len Bias, Bobby Ross, the popular winning football coach, departed to become head coach at Georgia Tech and went on to win a national championship there. His assistant coach, Joe Krivak, took over the position of head football coach at Maryland after the 1986 season. Joe was an old-school, no-nonsense coach and a role model for his team and community. He believed in the value of education and what athletics could contribute to developing his young men. Krivak was perhaps the last educator coach I worked with.

Chancellor Slaughter personally chose Bob Wade in 1986 from Baltimore Dunbar High School to coach Maryland's men's basketball program. He was the first African American head coach at an ACC school and a surprising pick according to most basketball pundits. There had been bitter animosity between the basketball coaches in the Baltimore inner city and Lefty Driesell, resulting in a near boycott of Black basketball players enrolling at Maryland. Slaughter sought to relieve that drought by hiring Wade, a local coaching legend. The University of Maryland was purported to be one of the best head coaching jobs in the country and in the best conference. The conference was fierce, and many suspected that Wade was not up to the challenge.

Hiring Bob Wade was a gamble. A jump from high school coach to ACC head basketball coach generated skepticism from the fan base. More so, Wade would have a steep learning curve for absorbing complicated NCAA recruiting legislation, expectations for speaking functions at alumni events, and staying on top of his team's academic performance. Though African American college head basketball coaches are more common today, Bob Wade was the first in the ACC and had the additional pressure of high expectations placed on him by members of his race. John Slaughter offered a lengthy explanation for hiring Wade over other candidates with more college experience. Wade was cited for having strong character, a history of academic commitment, a record of tremendous success in high school athletics, and an understanding of recruiting. He had coached players on John Thompson's championship Georgetown teams but publicly feuded with Lefty Driesell. Although some high school coaches had success in big-time college sports, it was not common. Wade was a former professional football player for the Baltimore Colts and Washington Redskins. He could have been a popular choice at Maryland, but Wade sensed that the athletic administration was against him so he rarely sought assistance. He believed that the new athletic director, Lew Perkins, was setting him up for failure. Wade was the personal choice of the chancellor but not the athletic director.

After the turmoil of Len Bias's death, Chancellor Slaughter insisted upon setting a new course for Maryland athletics.

In the fall of 1988—after working at Maryland for about a year—I was contacted by Donnie Duncan, my mentor and the former head football coach at Iowa State. Now the new athletic director at Oklahoma, Donnie wanted to hire me as the academic director there. I was flown down to Norman in November to attend the annual rivalry game between Oklahoma and Nebraska. There, I was introduced to a much grander college sports stage than I had been accustomed to. Although Oklahoma lost the game and its new star quarterback Charles Thompson broke his leg at the end, I witnessed two legendary coaches and programs clash in front of national television and eighty-five thousand fans. After the game, I was recruited by Barry Switzer to join the program. Switzer was very charming, and he took me to a bar to help him wind down after the game. The locale was a little awkward since I don't drink. Despite their efforts to hire me, I felt professionally obligated to Maryland, and my work was unfinished there. I declined the offer. As it turned out, my decision was fortuitous. A few months later, Oklahoma went on probation for major recruiting and extra-benefit violations, and Charles Thompson was arrested for selling cocaine. A spree of rapes, shootings in the athletic residence halls, and other violent crimes caused widespread embarrassment and forced Barry Switzer's resignation.[3]

Back at the University of Maryland in 1988, under the direction of Perkins, I shifted my primary attention from academics to Wade in my one-man compliance shop. I found a number of recruiting violations and a few of what I considered minor extra benefits for the players. Extra benefits included polo shirts given as Christmas gifts and allowing players to use the frequent flier miles they accumulated during game travel. Rather than feeling regret about my findings, Perkins was elated. He now had cause to report violations to the NCAA and fire Wade.

John Slaughter resigned from Maryland in 1988 to become president at Occidental College and was replaced by William (Brit) Kirwan. Brit, the former provost, was a popular choice at the University of Maryland. Shortly after Brit became chancellor at Maryland, I ran into him on campus and congratulated him. Kirwan made a remark that I remember well. He said something like, "Gerry, I observed in the *Chronicle of Higher Education* that nine of the last eleven college president resignations were related to athletic problems, and I don't intend on being one." Despite Kirwan's desire to avoid athletic scandals, he was repeatedly confronted with them at Maryland and later as president at Ohio State, yet he handled them well.

In May 1989, Bob Wade resigned. By June, Lew Perkins replaced Wade with Ohio State coach Gary Williams, who had returned to his alma mater. After turning over my findings about Wade to the NCAA, the university was sent an official letter of inquiry specifying the allegations of wrongdoing. In 1990, the university was invited to a session with the NCAA's Committee on Infractions at the luxurious Hotel Del Coronado in San Diego. The NCAA always conducts its business, including infractions hearings, in first-class facilities. Before the university appeared before the NCAA's Committee on Infractions, Chancellor Kirwan's chief legal counsel, Dennis Blumer, asked me to investigate an early practice violation. He was acting on a tip given by basketball players to Kirwan that Wade's replacement as head basketball coach, Gary Williams, had been conducting impermissible structured practices before the official start date. Kirwan had previously received complaints from players that these impermissible practices were being conducted, and he had asked Perkins to investigate it. Perkins had gone to Williams, who admitted to the supervised early practices. Perkins then asked Williams to discontinue the early practices and reported to Kirwan that there was nothing to the allegations. However, the practices continued.

After interviewing the basketball players, I determined that they were probably being truthful. I then interviewed Assistant Coach Billy Hahn, who revealed that Williams had directed him to supervise the early practices. I immediately reported the finding of violation to Perkins, who was in Hawaii with one of Maryland's teams. Perkins said that he would report the violation to the chancellor. I checked with Perkins weekly to verify that he had reported the violation to the chancellor. After the third check-in, it was obvious that Perkins was avoiding his responsibility, so I reported the violation to university legal counsel Blumer. I didn't understand at the time the significance of what could be considered a secondary violation. Perkins's initial failure to report the infraction to Kirwan caused a rift in their relationship and ultimately resulted in a failure to renew Perkins's contract. It would also create a rift in my relationship with Perkins and Williams. In their minds, I jeopardized their jobs.

Perkins suspected that I was uncomfortable with his maneuver to unseat Wade. What most upset me was the realization that Perkins was inconsistent in his handling of violations by Wade and Williams. His willingness to overlook Williams's indiscretions proved that he tolerated an atmosphere of rule-breaking when it applied to his chosen investment.

The all-day session in front of the NCAA Committee on Infractions was intimidating and grueling. Roy Kramer, the former athletic director at Tennessee and later the long-time commissioner of the Securities and Exchange Commission, chaired the committee. The Maryland group was humbled, and although I did not embarrass my athletic director, our relationship would never be the same. There was a finding of eighteen major infractions, all of which the university had reported to NCAA enforcement staff. Despite the university's full cooperation with the NCAA, the NCAA Committee on Infractions levied a three-year probation, a two-year ban on postseason play, cited the university for lack of institutional control, and ordered it to show cause on the forced resignation of Bob Wade. This meant that any NCAA institution would have to "show cause" to the NCAA to avoid being subject to additional sanctions by hiring this coach. In effect, it made Wade unemployable.[4] Maryland had to return the $361,000 earned from the 1988 basketball tournament.

Perkins had gotten his wish to replace Wade but at a tremendous cost to the university. Kirwan angrily protested that he considered the NCAA's penalties heavy handed and wondered whether he should have hired a law firm that specialized in representing schools before the Committee on Infractions. The committee required that Maryland report the findings of Gary Williams's practice violations. Publicly, the media wondered whether Maryland's athletic problems would ever end. Privately, Kirwan's administration wondered whether complete cooperation with NCAA enforcement staff yielded any benefit.[5]

Cooperating with the NCAA's enforcement staff has long been a question I've wrestled with. There are inconsistencies in penalties levied with very little (if any) relief given for cooperation. Cheating in college sports is pervasive, and NCAA's enforcement staff seem inept at uncovering violations regardless of how many are hired. The severity of penalties seems dependent upon the prevailing political winds. What appears obvious is that NCAA enforcement typically activates in response to media investigations. The media repeatedly shames the NCAA into action rather than NCAA enforcement staff taking the initiative to uncover serious violations. The media not only affects the course of NCAA investigations; it also plays an important role in legislative change. The NCAA and college presidents seem content to reap the rewards of big-time college sports regardless of the occasional disruption due to scandal. They react swiftly to scandals that make headlines and that shape public opinion about universities or the integrity of the NCAA.[6]

The concept of NCAA institutional control was not enacted until 1990.[7] Individuals were held responsible for rule violations if the institution had no knowledge of the violations. In the case of Bob Wade, it appeared to me that his demise and the NCAA probation were a combination of several factors. First, Wade was inexperienced regarding the expectations of and pressures on an ACC head basketball coach. Second, many of the Maryland faithful and administrators wanted him to fail. Third, there was little effort by the Maryland administration to assist Wade to succeed. Finally, Wade's pride did not allow him to seek or accept help. He remained on an island, and no one came to his rescue. After three years, Wade compiled a 36–50 record and resigned amid the findings of major infractions in recruiting and extra benefits to players.

The success of Maryland athletics rested on the fortunes of the men's basketball team, and Lew Perkins was a young, aggressive athletic director who felt impatient with Wade's lack of success and was determined that the outlook for basketball was poor. Perkins directed me to delve more deeply into the rules compliance of Wade's program. Perkins had an agenda to replace him, even if it meant putting the school on probation. He saw Wade as incapable of bringing long-term success to the Maryland program. Although Wade recruited well, Perkins considered other factors to be an impediment. Basketball was the university's premier sport. I never sensed that Perkins's differences with Wade were personal or racially motivated. College basketball was Perkins's specialty, and he was convinced that Wade could not be successful on the ACC stage.[8]

Nationally, 1990 was significant to college athletics thanks to the work of (Maryland alum) U.S. Representative Tom McMillen and Senator Bill Bradley. Both had been professional basketball players who were deeply concerned about the poor graduation rates of college athletes and the misleading graduation reports from the NCAA and College Football Association. McMillen and Bradley co-sponsored a bill passed into law known as the Student Right to Know Act. It was important to the public because, for the first time, it required the annual reporting of graduation rate comparisons with the institutions' student body. The results were rather alarming and, once again, the big-time college sports connection with education was in question. African American athletes in football and basketball were the most vulnerable. The Right to Know Act brought tremendous attention to the importance of graduating athletes. It was regarded by the athletic administration as an annoying diversion from the entertainment industry. On the day that graduation rate reports became public, college presidents from traditional football powers were momentarily embarrassed by the public scrutiny and headlines. Presidents would pontificate on the importance of graduating their athletes until the season started. Perhaps a blue-ribbon faculty committee would be carefully appointed with friendly faculty. Ultimately, little changed.[9]

Since its inception, poor federally mandated graduation rates have been a sore spot for the NCAA and specific athletics programs with low graduation rates. In 2005, the NCAA manufactured its own methodology for graduation rates called the "graduation success rate." By this measure, athletes who transfer from the institution while eligible under the NCAA are excluded from consideration, and transfers who join the institution, as well as freshmen admitted for the spring term, are included. The NCAA's standard raises the graduation rate by ten to fifteen

> The Student Right to Know and Campus Security Act (also known as the Student-Athlete Right to Know Act) mandated for the first time, against strong NCAA resistance, the public disclosure of graduation rates for college athletes. The act officially amended the Higher Education Act of 1965 (HEA) to require "any such institution which participates in HEA student assistance programs and which is attended by students receiving athletically related student aid to provide certain information with respect to the graduation rates of student-athletes. Includes information on race and sex under such requirement."[a] In addition, the act required institutions to report this information annually to the secretary of education and provide it to the student and the student's parents, guidance counselor, and high school coach when offering a potential student-athlete any athletically related student aid.

percentage points. The corporate bureaucrats at the NCAA work hard to enhance their image. They are quite skilled at it.[10]

Lew Perkins left Maryland in 1990 to take over as athletic director of the University of Connecticut. Andy Geiger from Stanford University replaced Perkins. Geiger saw his role as bringing stability to the athletics program. That year, Maryland tied Louisiana Tech at the Poulan Weed-Eater Independence Bowl. The following season was poor, however. This led Geiger to conduct a review of the football program and interview its players. Geiger wanted to control his revenue-generating programs. This diminished Head Football Coach Krivak's authority and caused him to resign.

Geiger supported Gary Williams, who actively campaigned against my continuance in the compliance role. Williams thought my presence in compliance threatened his program and that I was detrimental to his chances for success. Geiger agreed and removed me from compliance. Geiger then established a compliance-by-committee concept, essentially making everyone in the department responsible for compliance. He set up a departmental committee to handle compliance activities. I openly opined that if everyone is responsible then no one is responsible, and such a model is doomed to fail.

In January 1992, my differences with Geiger came to a head, and I was reassigned as an assistant to the provost under Bob Dorfman. My single-minded strong opinions about integrity in intercollegiate athletics had once again put me at odds with an athletic director. I have found that college coaches and athletic directors view staff as either for or against them. To them, there are no shades of gray—no complex issues that may cause differences of opinion. Dissent and freedom of expression are not tolerated well in athletics. Taking a path that may be considered at odds with a revenue-producing coach is considered treason. Neither athletes nor administrators are paid to think independently. Instead, they are to follow orders. It was clear to me that Geiger wanted Gary Williams to have free rein to grow the basketball fortunes at Maryland. Geiger left Maryland after three years to take the athletic director position at Ohio State. Gary Williams went on to become the conquering home-town hero at Maryland and led his team to the 2002 NCAA National Championship, retiring in 2011.

While working in the Office of the Provost, I was permitted time to recover from the five years I spent in compliance. Though tumultuous, learning the intricacies of the entire NCAA rulebook was a useful intellectual experience. I also learned how to carefully interview athletic personnel, boosters, and athletes. My work at the provost's office allowed me to research factors relevant to the retention of students. This research would be useful for the remainder of my career.

I remained at the provost's office for about one and a half years, working on academic advising and retention issues for the university before leaving for a position at the University of Oklahoma. After Maryland, I promised my wife that I would never again take on compliance responsibilities in an athletics program. I was convinced that cheating in athletics was pervasive and irreconcilable. Since the 1984 *NCAA v. Regents* antitrust case, television money flowed into college football and basketball. The stakes were so high for coaches and athletic directors that greed and ambition became the primary consideration. I concluded that college football and men's basketball coaches would go to nearly any extreme to maintain their ability to reap profits. Coaches were not only instant celebrities but now also wealthy celebrities. It was not enough to be respected by the university and local fan communities. The goal was to amass enormous personal gain. In this environment, the educational role of big-time sports at the university was grossly distorted as a collegiate model of amateurism. The notion of the college coach as an educator in Division I athletics was a fantasy. It was as if college athletics had been swallowed up by a hostile corporate takeover.

FIVE

OKLAHOMA'S POST-SWITZER ERA

Finding a Fit

Donnie Duncan, the athletic director at the University of Oklahoma (OU), called on me again in 1993. His academic director position had reopened. Under his direction, the Oklahoma program underwent significant changes. It had withstood probation, egregious scandals, and the resignation of Barry Switzer. Gary Gibbs, a former linebacker under Switzer, became the new Oklahoma head coach in 1989. Donnie and I had remained great friends, and he regarded me as the best in my field of athletic academic support. After visiting Oklahoma a second time, I accepted his offer. Oklahoma would become my new home, and I would once again be cast into a new athletic scandal.

Gary Gibbs probably had one of the most difficult jobs in college football. He followed an extremely popular and irrepressible legendary character in Barry Switzer. Players and fans loved his swagger and confidence. Not only did Switzer teams win often and win big, but they were known for overpowering their opponents. Generations of great players like Steve "Dr. Death" Williams, Brian Bosworth, Keith Jackson, the Selmon brothers (Lucious, Lee Roy, and Dewey), and Tony Casillas would manhandle opponents. Years earlier, I watched the Oklahoma team arrive at Iowa State. Even stepping off the bus, they looked intimidating. They were the kind of players you hoped would finish the game without causing major injury to your team. Beating Oklahoma's football team wasn't even a consideration.

OU was put on the map by the fortunes of its football program. It is the home of seven national championships and seven Heisman

Trophy winners. OU president from 1943 to 1968, George Lynn Cross once stated to the state legislature, "I want to build a university the football team can be proud of." Oklahoma Memorial Stadium is located near the center of campus, reminding all who visit campus of the importance of football to the university's image. Under Switzer, the fans expected wins and wouldn't tolerate mediocrity. OU fans expected their Sooners to hang "half a hundred" by halftime. The psyche of the Sooner fan base rested on the fortunes of its football team. The resignation of Switzer was a blow to the university, but its fans expected to continue to win big in football. Nevertheless, winning a national championship is always considered a possibility for Oklahoma, and everyone associated with the university community expected it of us.

Under the constraints of NCAA probation, Gary Gibbs worked tirelessly to win without running afoul of the NCAA rulebook. He managed to keep the Oklahoma program clean and go to bowl games. By the standards of almost any other university fan base, his record would have been enough. Winning the Big 8 Conference Championship but failing to beat Texas frustrated the spoiled fans. In Gibbs's final football season, I was on the field after a game and personally observed a fan spit on his face following a game. An airplane was rented to fly over the stadium during a game with a sign encouraging Gibbs to leave. OU fans wouldn't tolerate mere nine-win seasons. Going to what they considered minor bowls, such as the Gator Bowl or the Sun Bowl, was accepting mediocrity. Impatience for the OU program to recover from its penalties grew, and many called for Gibbs to resign. Although Gibbs never had a losing season—he went 44–23–2 as head coach and won two of three bowl games—ungrateful OU fans mounted a successful campaign to remove him. Gibbs took the honorable route and resigned.

While Gibbs was the head coach, he asked me to devise a system of routinely checking the class attendance of his athletes. Although the notion of spending resources to make certain that football players were attending class was appalling to me, I capitulated and organized a system of class checking. I had come to realize that when the head football coach requests a new approach, it was in your best interest to find a way to make it happen as quickly as possible. About $10,000 per semester was spent "bird-dogging" athletes. We employed retirees and students to unobtrusively determine whether athletes were present in their classes—routinely completing thirty-seven thousand checks per semester. It became a circus. Athletes would leave class as soon as the class checker departed, and those turned in for class absences would complain the checkers missed them.

Class-checking athletes has since become common practice across many campuses. The need for class checking indicates that some athletes do not value the opportunity for education afforded them—viewing college as a chore necessary to play their sport. In many cases, however, lack of academic motivation is due to athletes' lack of preparation for college, which can be a source of embarrassment that they would rather not expose in the classroom.[1]

If I had to pinpoint a moment when I felt certain that big-time college athletics had no place in higher education, it was my initiation to class checking at Oklahoma. Prior to that time, I recognized the need to reform college athletics but thought the existing model could be repaired. I was a true believer in the value of academic support in big-time

Hiring individuals to verify the class attendance of college athletes is a common occurrence. In the early 1990s, Gurney developed one of the most comprehensive class-checking systems in the NCAA. This system was eventually imitated by most every other school. Many schools see class checking as a way to encourage athlete attendance and consider it a best practice for enhancing academic success.[a] There were some academic successes attributed to ensuring athletes were in class or to punishing nonattendance. However, Gurney eventually regretted the system he created, stating, "If I had to do it all over again, I would certainly not do it. This is not how an educational opportunity for intercollegiate athletes is supposed to work. To actually waste money sending people to classes to make sure athletes are attending them borders on the absurd. It goes beyond babysitting. It's craziness."[b]

college sports. I believed that college athletics benefited the development of young athletes, that the activity built character, and that coaches were educators. I justified my role in athletics as making a difference in the lives of individual athletes.

The absurdity of having to force-feed an education to unwilling and/or underprepared athletes led me to believe that the current commercial model of NCAA athletics was an incurable cancer on higher education. At this point in my career, I had encountered many instances of cheating, corruption, and greed in big-time college sports, and I had finally learned the hard lesson that these instances were not isolated nor unrelated to the larger industry. This realization transformed me into a vocal, nationally recognized critic of the NCAA.

To approve of and fund class-checking efforts was professionally embarrassing. Nevertheless, class checking led to athletes' improved attendance and grades. Eligibility for competition improved because athletes were passing more classes. Though effective, class checking tended to humiliate the athletes who typically attended their classes, as well as the individuals employed to do the checking. Faculty must have thought that the athletics department had hit a new low—hiring, in effect, truancy officers for full scholarship students! At times, athletes checked for attendance created such distractions and disruptions in class that my advisers were forced to withdraw them from the classes to allow others to learn. It became obvious that my primary job was to protect the considerable investments made by the university to keep athletes on the field of play. Our titles could be couched in idealistic educational terms, but what was most important was keeping athletes eligible. A single athlete's loss of eligibility would be viewed as my personal failure regardless of whether I had any control over its occurrence. I was working within an entertainment enterprise that had a loose connection with education.[2]

The United States is the only country in the world that admits athletes to its finest universities without the necessary skills to compete academically with the rest of the student body. Everywhere else, students earn their places in higher education through academic merit and preparation; athletics is an extracurricular activity and high-level competition wherein games are presented through club sports. In the

United States, our public's obsession with winning attaches value to the reputations of its universities through victories on football fields or basketball courts. In spite of this folly, higher education embraces its role in quasi-professional sports and builds massive arenas with spectacular private suites and amenities for boosters to display their modern-day gladiators. The show must go on.

Upon my arrival at OU, I had the opportunity to design a unique model of academic support for college athletics. The College of Architecture, once housed in the stadium, was moved into a new facility, and my academic support unit was given room to grow. I hired terrific academic support staff, drawing experienced advisers from other universities. I also had a marvelous administrative assistant, Terri Moyer, who was wise beyond her years and knew everything and everyone at the university. She was invaluable.

Rather than the typical model of tutor rooms and study areas, I developed a novel learning center approach, which involved creating a collection of centers with specific foci: foreign languages, writing, computers, mathematics, career guidance, and academic advising. This model was a great success; it received national recognition and benefited OU recruiting. When recruits brought their parents to the athletics department, the parents were usually so impressed with the academic

Academic support services and academic advising for college athletes date back to the 1970s.[c] In those early years—prior to the development of standalone academic centers like Oklahoma's, which became a model for others—college athlete academic programs primarily consisted of one or two individuals. These individuals were mostly part-time or held additional full-time jobs and served as advisers tasked with maintaining athlete eligibility.[d] Often, these advisers were members of the coaching staff, which created pressure to enroll students in classes that ensured their eligibility rather than focusing on their graduation with a degree.[e] Over time, the need to maintain athlete eligibility has led to the establishment of multimillion-dollar athletic academic centers, all aimed at ensuring athletic eligibility.

center that we often signed the players. Other programs (e.g., LSU's Cox Center) emulated this model I developed at OU.

After the departure of Gary Gibbs, Donnie Duncan launched a search for OU's next head football coach, and I was appointed to the search committee considering several candidates. Donnie's first choice was Mack Brown at the University of North Carolina. Mack was Donnie's offensive coordinator at Iowa State, had been the offensive coordinator for Barry Switzer, and had head coaching experiences at Appalachian State and Tulane. I had remained friends with Mack since Iowa State, and was very excited by the prospect of him joining us. Donnie brought Mack and his wife, Sally, to OU President David L. Boren's home for an informal evening gathering to meet the search committee. Mack was charming and undoubtedly a great fit for OU. Donnie was able to get his commitment to be OU's next head coach, but, at the last minute, Mack asked to go back to North Carolina to think it over. Though I'm uncertain of his precise reasons, Mack later declined OU's offer.

As time went by, several other coaches were deemed unacceptable or declined our offers. As pressure mounted to name OU's new head coach so as not to lose recruits, Howard Schnellenberger emerged as an option. Donnie met Schnellenberger while at the National Football Foundation and Heisman Week festivities in New York in December 1994. Howard was a protégé of the great Bear Bryant and Don Shula, had won a national championship at Miami, and resurrected the Louisville program to respectability. He had the reputation of being an old-school coach with a tough work ethic and blue-collar mentality. Howard experienced many obstacles at OU, not the least of which was a clash of personalities between himself and President Boren. The flamboyant Howard Schnellenberger insisted on recognition of his celebrity for what he had accomplished before arriving at OU. Howard failed to recognize that OU's legendary football program was built largely upon coaches like Bud Wilkinson and Barry Switzer, who were given the opportunity to coach at Oklahoma and achieved phenomenal success.

The August 1995 summer preseason practice was one of the hottest on record in Oklahoma. For weeks, temperatures reached 100 degrees

Fahrenheit during two-a-day preseason practices. Instead of moving practices indoors or canceling altogether, Howard insisted on practicing outdoors. For several days, the weather was so intolerable that the training room was filled with athletes attached to intravenous fluid bags. One day, several football players collapsed and were sent to the hospital for heat stroke treatment. Two freshman athletes were seriously affected and never played again. One transferred from Oklahoma. The other worked as a student employee in my academic center for several years while pursuing his education on medical disability. His mental faculties were never the same after suffering heat stroke.

I don't believe Howard Schnellenberger's subpar 5–5–1 record at OU had anything whatsoever to do with his short, one-year tenure. Rather, Schnellenberger's clashes with President Boren and mistreatment of athletes sealed his fate at Oklahoma. Howard was Donnie Duncan's personal choice for OU's football coach, and President Boren held him accountable for his failure. After just one season, Donnie was searching for another head coach and, once again, I was appointed to the official search committee.

This time, President Boren took a more hands-on approach in selecting the next football coach. Boren sought guidance from Barry Switzer, who was head coach for the Dallas Cowboys at the time. Barry recommended his defensive line coach for the Cowboys and former player at OU, John Blake. Barry reasoned that Blake, an African American with Texas and Oklahoma ties, had the expertise to attract the best football recruits to OU. Blake, an OU graduate, had an interview with the committee, which included several faculty. Prior to the interview, it was made clear that Blake was the president's selection. Blake had no prior experience as a head coach at any level or as a coordinator. He appeared to be very nervous and struggled to find the answers to our questions. We left the interview knowing full well that his ascendancy to the responsibilities of Oklahoma's head coach would be very difficult.

John Blake's tenure as head coach was an example of a man out of his comfort zone. He sought solace through prayer and meditation. I often observed him reading the Bible in his office and on team flights to and from away games. Blake appeared nervous and lacked the confidence that those who follow Oklahoma football prefer a head coach exude. Although being the head coach at Oklahoma was obviously a dream of Blake's, it seemed as though he was waiting for the axe to fall and relieve him of the heavy burden. OU made an enormous effort to build Blake's people and decision-making skills; however, Blake did not embrace this effort. He surrounded himself with a staff of friends who were poor coaches and advisers. More experienced coaches on his staff chose to leave. After Blake's dismal first season of 3–8 in 1996, Donnie Duncan resigned to the newly created Big 12 Conference as senior associate commissioner in charge of football operations.

Donnie Duncan deserves a great deal of credit for guiding Oklahoma athletics through some of its most challenging years. The NCAA probation in 1988 took scholarships, television revenue, and three years of bowl game appearances from OU. This was harsh and designed to hurt the program. The subsequent year's disasters (rapes, shootings, and drug scandals) by OU football players led to the unpopular forced resignation of Barry Switzer. Donnie successfully held the OU athletic program together through the maelstrom. Managing a college athletic program is simple when success on the field brings regular conference and national championships, when money and accolades pour into campus. It is quite another matter to manage a giant struggle through scandal on one hand and an angry fan base on the other.

In 1996, President Boren selected Steve Owens to succeed Donnie Duncan as OU's athletic director. Steve, the 1969 Heisman Trophy winner (one of seven from OU), is extremely popular throughout Oklahoma. While at OU, Steve worked hard at bringing a business model to the management of the athletics department. Since the 1988 NCAA probation and the effect of television and bowl bans, OU was in debt. Steve cut staff and worked on cost reductions. This was an unusual position for OU; the program historically accepted no subsidies from the university or student fees.

In 1997, following a rare John Blake victory over twenty-third-ranked Syracuse, Steve and Barbara Owens returned home to learn their son Blake had died. This loss deeply affected the Owens family and made it impossible for Steve to concentrate on his work at OU. Steve resigned in 1998 for personal reasons. OU lost the considerable talents of someone I valued as an outstanding man and a potentially great athletic director. Once again, OU was in the market for an athletic director. In 1998, Joe Castiglione, the athletic director from Missouri, was chosen to succeed Steve Owens.[3]

John Blake continued to stumble through three painful years at OU—becoming further isolated on campus. Blake resigned in 1998, and the university settled his contract. After ten years of despair in the once legendary Oklahoma football program, we were once again in the position of searching for a new head coach.

THE FOOTBALL MESSIAH ARRIVES

Football-associated revenues power Oklahoma's athletic program and, by 1998, these revenues had dwindled. The program borrowed funding from the university each year and accumulated approximately $15 million in debt. The public wondered whether the University of Oklahoma (OU) would ever recover. It had been through three head football coaches in rapid succession, and all were considered failures by the fan base. Under John Blake, the once proud Sooners were perennial bottom dwellers.

Castiglione scoured the country for acceptable candidates to succeed Blake as OU head football coach. Two of Castiglione's assistant athletic directors at Oklahoma, Kirby Hocutt and Bruce Van De Velde, previously worked at Kansas State University and were familiar with Bob Stoops. Coach Stoops was the former defensive coordinator under legendary coaches Bill Snyder at Kansas State then Steve Spurrier at the University of Florida. Both Hocutt and Van De Velde were instrumental in coaxing Bob's interest in OU.[1] At the University of Florida, Bob Stoops earned a reputation as one of the hottest assistant coaches in the country. Stoops had helped his mentor Spurrier and the 1997 Florida Gators win the national championship. Hiring another unproven assistant coach was a gamble for Joe Castiglione, but Bob brought a substantial coaching pedigree, was young and personable, and had a great work ethic. Hiring Stoops renewed the faith of those Sooners who had abandoned the football religion. Bob hired the unconventional Mike Leach to lead his offense and Brent Venables and his brother, Mike Stoops, to lead his defense. Leach had been at Kentucky and ran a spread offense that gave fits to his Gators. Mike and Brent were at Kansas State working under Bill Snyder.

When Bob Stoops arrived on Oklahoma's campus, I ran into him and his wife, Carol, as they were touring the football facility. After introductions, I told Bob how badly stability was needed in our program. He was to be the fourth football coach I worked with in five years. I told him that my wish for Oklahoma was that he would "just stay." Coaching turnover can be disastrous for a program. From observing coaches come and go, my rule of thumb for any college sport is that, over a three-year period, about 30 percent of the athletes will leave due to a coaching change. The relationship developed among players, the head coach, and the coach that recruited the players, is so strong that it affects mutual confidence. Players from the previous regime are often evaluated as unable to compete for playing roles, become discouraged, and look for options at other schools. Bob promised to stay and kept his promise. The fortunes of Bob Stoops and Oklahoma football were about to change.

Despite hope on OU's horizon, the stressors of my career began catching up with me. In 1999, I suffered a heart attack. While working in my office, I began experiencing chest pain and shortness of breath. If it were not for the insistence of my administrative assistant, Terri Moyer, and our head trainer, Scott Anderson, I would not have gone to the hospital. Their quick assessment and actions saved my life.

Later that same year, I was able to get approval to name my academic center after my mentor, Prentice Gautt. Though the center wasn't fancy by today's standards, its thirty-thousand square feet offered us a quiet, spacious area in the stadium for athletes to pursue their education and remediation. Normally, athletic facilities are named after wealthy donors who contribute money for naming rights. Prentice was not a donor. I was proud to have taken part in naming our facility after Prentice for his lifetime achievements as the first African American football player at OU. Seeing Prentice's sincere appreciation was a profound honor for me. It was my hope that Prentice's name on the academic center would remind future generations of where hard work and sacrifice in the pursuit of academics could take them.

Gerald Gurney, David Boren, Sandra Gautt, Prentice Gautt, Don Halverstadt, and Joe Castiglione at the University of Oklahoma football halftime for dedication of the Prentice Gautt Academic Center, 1999. *University of Oklahoma Athletics*

In 2003, I had the pleasure of nominating Prentice Gautt for an honorary doctorate at OU. Prentice received the doctorate at graduation that year in honor of his bravery in integrating OU athletics and the Southwest region of the nation. I gave his nomination speech at the dinner honoring the winners. Although I have had many professional achievements in my career, I consider these to be among my greatest.[2]

In December 1999, an important class action lawsuit raged through the federal Third Circuit Court of Appeals challenging NCAA rules on freshman competitive eligibility and the ability to earn an athletic scholarship. *Cureton v. NCAA* specifically challenged the requirement that incoming college athletes achieve a minimum score on either of two standardized tests (SAT or ACT) as a condition of eligibility to participate in intercollegiate athletics and/or to receive athletically related financial aid during their freshman years.[3] The plaintiffs claimed that since African Americans were more likely to be ineligible by virtue

Athletic academic centers have become much more opulent and an important part of the college sports arms race to—at least ostensibly—demonstrate a commitment to academics. Several institutions now have multimillion-dollar athlete-only academic support centers that are used as a primary recruiting tool to sell the "student-athlete first" mantra, which many consider more of a myth than true educational primacy. One major issue is who supervises and runs these centers. More often than not, the academic advisers are paid and supervised by that athletics department and, in some cases, coaches are supervising. The conflict of interest is stark when the eligibility of an athlete is in question. Rarely do academic advisers win those arguments. Institutions often do whatever it takes to keep an athlete on the field of play. Many have called for athletic academic advisement to be housed, supported, and supervised outside of the athletics department. Some institutions have done this, but most athlete academic centers remain under the control of the athletics department. Many organizations and even the NCAA support having these operations under the control of an academic entity.[a]

of test score requirements, the NCAA was violating Title VI of the 1964 Civil Rights Act, which precluded racial discrimination in any program receiving federal financial aid.

The Third Circuit Court of Appeals overturned the decision of the federal district court in Philadelphia, which initially provided relief to the named plaintiffs, Tai Kwan Cureton, Leatrice Shaw, Andrea Gardner, and Alexander Wesby. The plaintiffs represented a group of African American college athletes suing on the basis that the NCAA's initial-eligibility rules had a disparate impact on minority athletes.[4] The appeals court found the NCAA's initial-eligibility rules exempt because it was not receiving federal aid. For a brief time before the case was overturned, football and basketball coaches saw an opportunity for open access to underprepared, talented athletes without a minimum score of 17 for the ACT or 820 for the SAT. A finding for the plaintiffs would have opened the floodgates to many great athletes unprepared for college work. Despite a successful appeal, college presidents advised the

Prentice Gautt and Gerald Gurney at the University of Oklahoma honorary doctorate ceremony, 2003. *University of Oklahoma Athletics*

NCAA that future initial-eligibility requirements should open access to minorities. In just a few more years, coaches could bring virtually anyone to the doorsteps of the university, and their loyal administration would devise ways to keep them there.

Despite John Blake's shortcomings as a head coach, he recruited good football players who became the foundation of Bob Stoops's ascension to coaching stardom. It takes a broad skill set for big-time college coaches to be successful. Bob Stoops had them all. He had nerves of steel. Bob could sit on the sidelines before a game against rival University of Texas, having casual conversations. He wasn't afraid to take risks, although he ordered more risky plays early in his career at Oklahoma.

What I admire most about Bob is that he's a regular person despite his celebrity. To Stoops's great credit, he took personal responsibility for academic issues that arose. He preferred that I dealt directly with him on academic issues and disciplinary problems rather than naming an assistant coach as an academic liaison. He recognized the importance of the academic performance of his athletes. Unlike most academic directors, I had direct and immediate access to Stoops when I needed to see him. I made it clear that when I asked to see him, I had something important to talk to him about. I was not interested in wasting Bob's time, and it was in his interest to deal with the issue at hand.

With the help of talented staff, Bob's first-season team won more than it lost and went to the Independence Bowl. Mike Leach found a disciplined, tough quarterback from Snow Junior College named Josh Heupel.[5] Opponents found Leach's version of the new spread offense befuddling. The offense was so successful that Leach landed the head coaching job at Texas Tech after Stoops's first season. I missed Leach. He was unconventional compared to most coaches. He had not played college football and, after college, went to law school at Pepperdine. His interests extended beyond football, and I enjoyed talking to him about literature and politics. The offense was taken over by the very capable offensive line coach, Mark Mangino, who later took Kansas to the Orange Bowl.

Oklahoma ushered in the millennium with its seventh national championship, and Bob Stoops took his place beside Bud Wilkinson and Barry Switzer in Sooners history. The early football polls prior to and during the 2000 season ranked the Sooners nineteenth. We steadily climbed as we played through the schedule. By midseason, the third-ranked Sooners were to play their old rival and first-ranked Nebraska Cornhuskers at home. The evening before the game, Castiglione launched a $125 million campaign to renovate the stadium and build facilities for other sports. During the reception, spirits were high, and Stoops assured the fans a victory. The following day, he and his team made good on the promise and won a thrilling victory on national television. Nebraska scored the first two touchdowns. The Sooners came roaring back with thirty-one unanswered points. Sooner magic had returned, and money came pouring into the athletics department coffers. OU breezed through the remainder of the season with Texas A&M and our in-state rival Oklahoma State, giving OU its only serious challenges.

After a thrilling win over Kansas State in the Big 12 Championship in Kansas City's Arrowhead Stadium, we were invited to play against Bobby Bowden's Florida State Seminoles team in the first BCS championship held at the Orange Bowl. My wife, daughter, brother Nelson, and best friend Norman Shafran joined me in watching our Oklahoma Sooners capture a hard-fought 13–2 victory in Miami. The thrill of being a part of a national championship team was numbing. Sitting in Pro Player Stadium at the end of the game, staring at the scoreboard, I simply couldn't believe I had a part in this spectacle.

We left Miami on a chartered plane with the team. When we arrived in Oklahoma City, eight Oklahoma state police cars escorted our team buses for the short trip to Norman. In the early hours of a cold January morning, fans lined our return route and cheered as we rode past. Television helicopters filmed our arrival for live telecast. When we pulled into Norman, the bus took an unusual departure from our typical drop-off point. Instead, we pulled into the stadium to greet five thousand adoring fans waiting for a glimpse of our conquering heroes. OU had returned to its customary spot on top of college football and Bob Stoops was ordained the University of Oklahoma's new messiah.

Winning a football championship requires great talent, dedication to a single-minded purpose, and an element of luck. What I remember most about that team was the scarcity of highly recruited stars and the genuine camaraderie among the members of the team. One of my favorite football athletes on that team was Renaldo Works. He was raised in Tulsa, Oklahoma, by hardworking parents. His father was a firefighter, and his mother was a letter carrier for the postal service. Both wanted their children to have a better life than they had. Renaldo played running back and had a stellar career at Oklahoma, but what I admired most about Renaldo was his determination to take advantage of his time at OU in order to leave with a quality education. Renaldo exceeded academic expectations after enormous effort and full utilization of the academic support system at OU. In his senior year at OU, he was named one of eleven National Football Foundation and College Hall of Fame Scholar-Athletes and was awarded a postgraduate scholarship. After earning a spot on the Houston Texans professional football team, Renaldo returned to Oklahoma a couple of years later to finish his schooling in a competitive business major. Once his undergraduate degree was complete, Renaldo earned an MBA from OU's Price College of Business. He then became an executive for the Conoco-Phillips Corporation.

Joe Castiglione, Renaldo Works, Bob Stoops, and Gerald Gurney at the 2003 National Football Foundation and College Hall of Fame Banquet at the Waldorf Astoria in New York City

Renaldo is an example of the NCAA's successful advertising campaign that emphasizes that the majority of NCAA athletes go "pro" in something other than sports.[6] He is an individual who took full advantage of the opportunity of an education. Despite devoting forty-six hours per week to football-related activities while in college, Works persevered and succeeded even with the odds stacked against him. He earned a promising future. Renaldo's story is what college athletics can and should be: a deserving young man's efforts in football and academic life resulted in a promising future. His story resonates as a throwback to days past.

SEVEN

THE COLLEGE SPORTS ARMS RACE

Most of the athletes on Oklahoma's football championship roster were not five-star recruits. They were tough, determined young men with a dogged work ethic. Oklahoma's national championship drew the attention of five-star recruits from Texas and around the nation. Winning brought exceptional talent accompanied by entitled egos on the field and in the classroom. The new stars coming to Norman were primarily concerned with playing time and their preparation for the NFL draft. The Oklahoma Athletics Department supported this fantasy by building monuments to the football gods in an explosion of new and renovated facilities. Oklahoma Memorial Stadium became the Gaylord Family Memorial Stadium and received a complete renovation. The newly constructed Barry Switzer Center, which contained a new locker room and coaching offices, was gutted and rebuilt because it wasn't quite lavish enough. The football complex became a monument to players who won trophies and became professional athletes. The locker room was resplendently furnished with special oak lockers, a player lounge, leather furniture, pool tables, and big-screen televisions for video games to relax and entertain the players. The Siegfried family built a lavish strength facility with the best training paraphernalia money could buy.[1]

Nothing in the new OU football complex could possibly remind one that it existed within a university or that it was affiliated with an *educational* institution. Donations continued to pour in, and the university's capital fundraising campaign exceeded its goal. Other sports at the university benefited from the football championship. A soccer facility and field, tennis courts, and softball and golf improvements rapidly appeared. Every sport profited from the win with some sort of facility improvement.

A grateful OU president and board of regents handsomely rewarded their coach before the season ended. After the stunning win over Nebraska in 1999, Bob Stoops's salary doubled from $700,000 to $1,400,000. At the end of the year, Bob's loyalty extended to his strength and conditioning staff and his assistant coaches, who also received boosts in wages.

One of the most pitiful spectacles I have observed in college athletics is when a revenue sports head coach loses his job. The one or two new dealer cars, gasoline cards, clothing allowance, free meals at restaurants, free private jet travel, and numerous other amenities in their lives are removed. Coaches become so accustomed to the luxury and celebrity bestowed upon them that they often find it difficult to adjust to buying their own meals, purchasing a private vehicle, flying commercial, and buying their own clothes. Although a smart head coach usually accumulates enough savings to live comfortably, life after coaching is even more difficult for assistant coaches. Mundane daily tasks, which the public does regularly to maintain existence, become a new challenge for coaches who are no longer in favor. If unable to find another job in college or professional coaching, they may face a tough job market unless an alumnus takes pity and hires them. Head coaches often get picked up as color commentators on game days to supplement their incomes. But alas, the inflated salaries for coaches are designed to compensate them for the risks they take. Coaches are accustomed to being fired and hired. The millions of dollars accumulated, due to having nearly no expenses, provide a comfortable cushion to land upon.

Bob Stoops's agent, Neil Cornrich, got outstanding results for his client.[2] Aside from the usual amenities, lavish bonuses amounting to millions of dollars were negotiated into Stoops's contract for staying at Oklahoma. These bonuses were for delivering a winning season (including bowl games and winning against Texas), top-ten finishes, and so on. Academic incentives, for which his students may or may not achieve, were structured into his income.[3] Oklahoma, like other schools that wanted to boost coach compensation, looked for any incentive that might be achieved in order to augment Stoops's salary.[4] After all, it is essential to keep their beloved coach in Norman, where stadium season tickets will be renewed and donations will grow. Through the singular hire of Bob Stoops, Athletic Director Joe Castiglione earned his own brand of celebrity.

With the capital fundraising campaign goals exceeded, ongoing building and renovation of facilities, and a significant profit in the operating budget, Castiglione parlayed Stoops's success into a fortune for himself. Castiglione suddenly became one of the nation's most successful and influential athletic directors. He also used his marketability and notoriety to secure an enormous raise and one of the highest salaries in the nation for an athletic director. Money was spread everywhere in football, from the head coach to the strength and conditioning coaches. On the other hand, the academic support staff, who are responsible for the eligibility and academic progress of the players, received raises commensurate with university employees. In 2003, the stadium academic center received a facelift along with all the administrative offices on the stadium's north end. Although the existing center was adequate, keeping a fresh appearance to attract recruits was important.[5]

For the university and athletics department, 2003 was a banner year in other ways. *USA Today* and the NCAA awarded OU an academic achievement award. Our 73 percent graduation rate significantly exceeded that of our student body, leading the Big 12 Conference in overall graduation rate and in football. The graduation rate for our specially admitted population of marginalized students was 65 percent. President Boren used OU's honor and graduation rates in short ads for the university, which played during televised games.

Myles Brand replaced Cedric Dempsey as president of the NCAA in 2003. As president of Indiana University, Brand achieved notoriety for firing Bob Knight, Indiana's fiery and popular men's basketball coach. His ascendancy to NCAA leadership signified that college presidents had taken control of this large bureaucracy—the assumption being that college presidents would restore academic integrity to the much-maligned college sports industry. Upon his arrival at the NCAA, Myles Brand's primary platform was academic reform and ensuring that

In June 2003, the University of Oklahoma was one of thirty-two programs in Division I-A to be honored by the American Football Coaches Association for posting a graduation rate of more than 70 percent. In a halftime presentation in the fall of 2003, Dutch Baughman (executive director of the Division I-A Athletics Directors Association) presented Athletic Director Joe Castiglione and Gerald Gurney with the award.

The University of Oklahoma Board of Regents presented the entire academic staff with the Award of Excellence, 2003

academic primacy was a priority in college sports. Later that same year, Brand set out to develop what would become his legacy at the NCAA—academic integrity, or at least the attempt to establish it. Whether he was effective is up for debate. Initially, Brand persuaded the NCAA membership to set new initial-eligibility standards designed to provide access to higher education and raise eligibility standards. A sliding scale for initial eligibility was set that theoretically made it possible for an athlete to answer zero questions correctly on the ACT or SAT if the athlete scored a high grade point average (GPA); alternatively, the recruited athlete could have a very low GPA if the athlete somehow had a high entrance exam score. By finding benevolent teachers who would pass them, talented high school athletes could establish eligibility without any learned academic skills or accumulated knowledge. Their high school coaches would see to it, by hook or by crook, that the most talented athletes received the grades necessary to play in college.[6]

If the athlete's high school insisted on maintaining its integrity, there were always diploma mills and courses to supply the grades needed—for a price. For example, Pete Thamel and Duff Wilson of the *New York Times*[7] discovered the University High School—a correspondence school where, for $399, grades and courses were manufactured and placed on transcripts for athletes seeking college eligibility. The handlers of talented athletes devised ingenious means of getting their students a chance to go to college. Despite having a large staff evaluating transcripts daily, the NCAA Eligibility Center missed these correspondence schools. In their typical fashion, after being exposed by the media, the NCAA's leadership expressed shock at this dastardly act of academic dishonesty and vowed to restore honor to higher education. The NCAA then searched high and low to disqualify transcripts from the several schools already identified by the *New York Times*.[8]

The wheels of reform at the NCAA churn slowly unless a scandal makes a mockery of intercollegiate athletics. In the face of media exposure, the NCAA's public relations machine initiates damage control and acts quickly. In the case of correspondence schools and academic dishonesty, the NCAA designed an elaborate smokescreen to leave the public with the impression that NCAA leadership had restored academic integrity to college athletics. Walter Harrison, president of the University of Hartford, chaired a committee on academic reform that devised an obtuse metric for eligibility and retention called the academic progress rate (APR). Under the Academic Performance Program, an athlete could earn a point for retention and a point for eligibility each semester, for a total of four points per academic year. Each team was evaluated based on the ratio of points earned to potential points. If a team's score fell below the threshold that indicated a 50 percent federal graduation rate, the wrath of the NCAA would come down with a nasty public letter of reprimand and the loss of financial aid allotments. Lower scores would require tougher penalties, including loss of postseason play. Such efforts might be admirable if the public understood or valued this elaborate new program. However, the scores are difficult to evaluate and easy to manipulate, and the public largely regards the APR as a meaningless metric. This effort by the NCAA is a classic bait-and-switch tactic to manipulate academic integrity while trying to present it positively to the public.[9]

By 2008, the NCAA's research unit declared that an APR of 925 predicted a 37 percent federal graduation rate.[10] It became obvious that colleges with resources could manipulate the system to ensure they would not be penalized. Schools that had limited resources would suffer NCAA penalties. Each year, the NCAA would release its APR numbers with much fanfare. Oklahoma's football team would have an APR of 943, Maryland's a 939, SMU's a 956, and Iowa State's a 939. The public would be left scratching their heads and wondering what this nonsense was all about and whether their favorite team's running back would be eligible for the fall season. Embarrassed by the obvious failure of its Academic Progress Program, the NCAA set new standards and revised its punitive measures. In the NCAA's classic fashion of shaping its image, it set a standard of 930 to presumably predict a 50 percent graduation success rate rather than its original federal graduation rate.[11] The NCAA-manufactured graduation success rate tends to be about 15 percentage points higher than the federal graduation rate.[12]

The NCAA's threatened punitive measures have spurred the growth of fancy academic centers for athletes, dramatically increased expenditures on programs to keep athletes eligible, and encouraged the practice of clustering athletes into easy majors such as general studies, sports management, interdisciplinary studies, multidisciplinary studies, and so on. This practice is designed to maintain athletes' eligibility and graduate them in quasi-academic programs without sufficient academic rigor. The advertised academic success of big-time athletics has come at a tremendous cost to higher education.[13]

Winning the football national championship brought a new recruiting philosophy to the University of Oklahoma. The coaching staff sought to sign the top recruits in the nation. Five-star recruits from Texas and across the country became the goal for each recruiting class. It became increasingly apparent that most of the recruits were focused on professional football careers. Earning a degree was a secondary consideration. Unlike my experiences at Iowa State, SMU, and Maryland,

Oklahoma Sooners football players were, first and foremost, preparing for and expecting professional careers in football.

Even though colleges poured large sums of money into educational support, fancy academic centers, and financial aid, many football athletes opted to do only what was necessary to maintain their eligibility. Failing and repeating courses was commonplace. Taking remedial mathematics up to seven times until the players were drafted was typical. Over time, I concluded that Oklahoma's tradition of winning football championships shaped and attracted the kind of students who valued the school as a training ground for player development and preparation for a career in professional football. As the years progressed, Oklahoma had remarkable success in winning and participating in national championships and bowl games. The media exposure ensured that a multitude of Oklahoma players would win prestigious awards and enter the professional ranks. Advised of their potential draft picks, many chose to leave college early. This pattern would perpetuate the interest of new prized recruits each year who would replace those Oklahoma players leaving early for the pros.

I created what is recognized by many to be the finest academic support program for college athletes in the nation. Unfortunately, it was only useful to those who took advantage of its services. I make a distinction between obtaining a degree and an education. Whether or not college athletes are prepared for the academic rigors of the classroom, their opportunities to take advantage of a meaningful education are limited by the time and physical effort committed to the sport. The NCAA estimates that a football player commits, on average, more than forty hours per week to athletic-related activities outside of school and study time.[14] With weightlifting scheduled for 6:00 a.m., conditioning or practice in the afternoon, time spent in the training room for taping or rehabilitation, and various meetings, finding time for academic pursuits—such as reading recommended books or attending school-sponsored events—is challenging even for the most academically capable athletes. For those who struggle academically, it can feel nearly impossible to balance these demands.

For the highly recruited and less academically talented athlete, competing in the classroom can be far more challenging and, at times, personally humiliating. After 2003, the NCAA's initial-eligibility standards increased access to colleges and universities for athletes—even those woefully academically underprepared. Athletes could be admitted with very low standardized test scores when accompanied by a sliding scale of high school grades. As one might expect, the academic rigor of high schools varies a great deal, and many athletes enter the university with inflated grades based on attendance and good behavior. Due to the lowered standards after 2003, the number of specially admitted students increased about 20 percent and, at times, constituted most prospective college athletes admitted to OU.[15] As the number of specially-admitted athletes increased, there was a corresponding decline in athletes' academic preparedness, as indicated by test scores. The university was admitting athletes who were fully qualified by NCAA standards but who read at elementary school levels.

The NCAA standards had gone full circle since my days at Iowa State when a 2.0 GPA sufficed. Proposition 48 and minimum test score standards that established minimal competencies returned us to a system that allowed nearly open admissions for the most underprepared recruits. Oklahoma and its competitors in the Big 12 Conference were accepting athletes who qualified at these new minimal and easily manipulated academic eligibility standards. This was the case with most institutions around the country. Winning was and is the priority, not education.

The reading specialists and team of licensed psychologists I employed confirmed that the numbers of functionally illiterate athletes and those admitted with learning disabilities were rising dramatically. I was proud that Oklahoma felt an institutional responsibility to remediate athletes, but I was concerned that the main function of the new NCAA standards was primarily to enable football to become more attractive to the entertainment business and television.

In 2008, with the review and approval of Athletic Director Joe Castiglione, I began a campaign of writing commentaries focusing on the need to toughen academic standards for athletes. Castiglione agreed with my conclusion that academic standards needed to be stronger. The two most widely circulated higher education trade journals, *Chronicle of Higher Education* and *Inside Higher Education*, were my primary platforms. I authored or coauthored articles such as "Stop Lowering the Bar for College Athletes,"[16] "A Better Way to Measure Coaches' Wins and Losses,"[17] "It's Time for the NCAA to Get It Right,"[18] "Now We Must Reform Athletics Reform,"[19] "Professors Must Speak Out: College Can No Longer Afford Athletics as Usual,"[20] and "Toughen NCAA Standards for Freshmen."[21] Such works contributed to a renewal of the national debate on the preparedness of athletes, the NCAA's academic reform efforts, and initial-eligibility standards.

I was particularly critical of the NCAA's propagandistic approach as more of a business plan than an academic performance initiative. I was also critical of the faculty athletic representative (FAR) role in college sports. These faculty members represent themselves as the guardians of academic integrity in college athletics while egregious academic dishonesty and major infraction cases doubled in the last decade.[22] Finally, I criticized college presidents' lack of leadership in intercollegiate athletics. I described them as miserable failures in their half-hearted attempts to repair big-time college sports. Later in my career, while serving in my role as a faculty member, I enjoyed freedom of expression in the classroom and beyond; however, as a senior member of athletic administration, I am confident that my views did not endear me to the president, athletic director, or FAR. Over time, I became an outspoken critic of the NCAA and college presidents' inability to control the corrosive effect of college athletics on higher education.

EIGHT

THE GREAT MAGICAL MYTH OF COACHING

As Oklahoma football prospered in the new millennium by winning championships, Coach Bob Stoops continued to receive substantial raises. With each conference championship and ascendancy to four national championship games, a grateful president and board of regents bestowed new contracts to avoid the possibility of Stoops leaving Norman for more lucrative opportunities. When Steve Spurrier left the University of Florida for the NFL Washington Redskins, Stoops was heavily recruited by boosters and administrators to return to the University of Florida. Each year, rumors from the national coaching carousel would abound, circulated by the media and agents of college coaches, and Stoops was frequently a leading candidate for vacant positions. The thought of losing our head coach was unbearable to the president, his administration, and the board of regents. This panic prompted a quick enhancement of Bob's salary. Over a decade's time, Bob's salary exploded fivefold to about $5 million. Of course, the University of Texas couldn't have its championship coach, Mack Brown, making less. Soon Mack's salary exceeded Bob's. The same salary enhancements happened for Pete Carroll at Southern Cal. When the Southeastern Conference schools (e.g., Florida, Louisiana State, and Alabama) began their succession of championships, their coaches' compensations for gridiron success (or promises of success) shattered rationality. Winning coaches portrayed a mystique that was rare and precious. College presidents—under pressure from the coaches' agents, boosters, and their boards—were urged to open their universities' coffers to steal or keep these Houdini-like winners.

As football head coaches prospered, so did assistant coaches, athletic directors, and college presidents. A similar escalation occurred throughout the coaching profession in basketball, softball, baseball, and other featured sports. Soon our men's and women's basketball coaches were enjoying exorbitant salaries based on the accomplishments of their athletes.

The University of Oklahoma was one of only a dozen or so universities that made a profit without support from the university's operating funds or student fees.[1] However, most athletic administrations rob the university and its students of much-needed funding for educational expenses to pay for coaching salaries. The college athletic enterprise, enjoying nonprofit status, commits about 35 percent of its revenue to coaching and administrative salaries.[2] The public would likely refrain from contributing to any other charities if they had similar administrative costs. In classic cartel fashion, the financial compensation for college athletes is restricted to the value of their athletic scholarships, while coaches are free to stuff their pockets.

The college sports entertainment extravaganza has little, if any, connection with educating American athletes. Coaches have perpetrated a destructive myth of American higher education, and college presidents have bought this lie. College administrators justify coaches' salaries by saying they are based on what the market will bear. It seems to me, however, that this inflated market is on the backs of athletes who do not receive their fair value from the millions in generated revenues.[3]

Ninety-eight percent of NCAA athletic programs are not able to cover their costs via external revenue sources and are heavily subsidized. These subsidies primarily come from student fees and other general fund sources, which are rising at a rate much higher than tuition.[a] Consequently, funding allocations to athletics directly affect college affordability for the general student body. Recent studies show significant increases in the percentage of athletics departments' income from student fees and institutional subsidies, amounting to billions of dollars annually.[b]

Although superstar coaches play a unique role in bringing visibility to their institutions, their positive contributions have become increasingly tainted by scandal as big-time programs have transformed into businesses that look more like entertainment than education. This has had a corrosive effect on every aspect of student-athletes' recruitment, retention, and graduation.

A more fair and accurate valuation of coaches would be based, at least in part, on the academic performance and graduation of their student-athletes.[4] By adopting and enforcing such a standard, academic institutions underline academics as a central, not tangential, part of student-athlete success. This standard would also provide valuable information to recruits and their families as they weigh decisions regarding where to attend college.

The idea that coaches should be held accountable for the academic success or failures of the students they recruit differs significantly from NCAA regulations and federal graduation measures, which have done little to change the culture of recruiting for football and men's basketball. The NCAA punishes academic institutions rather than establishing shared accountability with coaches. There are little to no incentives for coaches to be concerned about the academic life of their student-athletes beyond eligibility to play.

Although a coach is not the only factor contributing to the academic success of a student-athlete, coaches do play a very important role in choosing prospective student-athletes and judging their fitness to succeed academically at their institutions. Head coaches gauge their institutions' priorities and academic demands, select recruits, and convince those athletes of the fit between their academic preparedness and the institution's academic expectations. Head coaches also establish the culture of a team, including whether student-athletes will be judged based on their academic achievements as well as their athletic contributions. It is confounding and unacceptable that coaches, arguably the most important people in the college athletics arena, are awarded solely on their win-loss records, without consideration of their impacts on the academic success of their athletes.

Coaches wishing to rise in the ranks typically use jobs at mid-major, steppingstone institutions to recruit student-athletes with promising athletic abilities but little academic promise or fit with the institutions. After establishing winning records, those coaches then leave those institutions and student-athletes behind for more lucrative positions elsewhere. Often these students fail to graduate or reach graduation facing significant stress and challenges. For those who believe that there is inherent academic justification for athletics in colleges, coaches' compensation and priorities should reflect this. Institutions should implement standards of accountability that motivate academically responsible behavior in the best interest of its athletes.

NINE

THE "EDUCATIONAL EXPERIENCE"

Most of the athletes I worked with were striving to carve out an education that would prepare them for employment after sports. However, for many University of Oklahoma (OU) football, men's basketball, and baseball players, the primary goal was to prepare for a professional career in sports. Coaches felt entitled to treat their athletes as professionals and had little respect for their need to devote time to education or personal lives. Thus, these athletes were generally not active participants in their education. Instead, many settled for an educational experience based on hanging around campus and enjoying the celebrity of being a University of Oklahoma Sooners athlete. They were semi-students training very hard for their athletic careers while avoiding challenging academic work.

One aspect of being a celebrity Oklahoma football or men's basketball player was sexual promiscuity. As a consequence, a number of male athletes either came to the university as parents or fathered children while in school. One celebrated OU football player, who went on to play for the NFL, United Football League, and Arena Football League, sired five children with four women. The pattern of fatherhood became so concerning that Coach Stoops asked for increased programming on sex education. This issue also became a problem in the academic center, where many football players needed to participate in child-rearing activities instead of focusing on their academic work and remediation. We faced a choice between having athletes miss essential academic support or offering childcare. We chose to provide childcare to help improve their academic performance.

Football and men's basketball coaches prefer athletes dedicated to the business of their sport. Most college athletes are aware of coaches' expectations of hard physical training and willingly accept that responsibility. These athletes believe their coaches are helping them fulfill their dreams of a career in professional sports. They come to a university to receive competent technical training in their sport, strength and conditioning, and television exposure in exchange for their natural athletic talent. From the moment they arrive on campus as recruits, the message is clear: Oklahoma Athletics is about winning and getting to the NFL or NBA.

Across from the football stadium are bronze statues of each Heisman Trophy winner and OU's legendary coaches. A walk through the football facility includes a museum honoring players in professional football and award winners as well as awards such as Heisman and bowl trophies. The football offices and locker facilities all contain large, action portraits of former Stoops players in their professional uniforms. Portraits of former all-American football players are hung in the stadium's Santee Lounge for the fans to worship. In every direction, there are daily reminders of Oklahoma's tradition of building great players.

In a sense, Oklahoma's approach is honest, and players understand why they are recruited. Like many big-time sports programs, Oklahoma's chief draw for football and men's basketball recruits is the tradition of winning, television exposure, and success in getting their athletes into professional programs; it is not the reputation of its botany program, for example. Recruits choose to be part of the coaches' system, and the rules are very strict. I often hear that unscrupulous college recruiters victimize athletes. However, most football and basketball players at OU fully understand the system of serfdom they are about to enter. Athletes at OU are expected to graduate early from high school if they can, enroll at the university in the spring of their high school senior year, and fully commit to football and basketball's assigned training routines for the remainder of their college years. This also includes every summer, when they receive room and board funding for taking classes while they train in strength and conditioning.

When I began in college athletics, athletes who were academically eligible to play would get summer jobs or work at internships. Today, most notably across all major college sports institutions, including Oklahoma, nearly all athletes go to summer school to train for the ensuing season and as a way to catch up or get well academically.[1] Unfortunately, many athletes still did not feel the need to take advantage of the academic opportunity to study for or pass their entire summer schedule. The Oklahoma Athletics Department wasted hundreds of thousands of dollars each summer on dropped courses. The athletes' expressed attitude was that summer term compensation for room and board was payment for training. At Oklahoma, in the sports of football and men's basketball, summer enrollment was not voluntary.

For many football and men's basketball players who attended OU, attaining a degree was an inconsequential secondary consideration to their goals of becoming professional athletes. Going to classes was a necessary requirement to maintain their eligibility. For many, attending class was viewed as a hurdle, like spring football practice, that they needed to endure to play. The opportunity to take advantage of a quality education, to prepare for a career other than athletics, and to think critically was an ethereal notion that many did not embrace.

The vast majority of football and men's basketball players were admitted to OU under special exceptions and were woefully underprepared for competition in the classroom. In response, the academic support division's primary effort switched from academic supplementation to learning skill remediation.[2] In 2006, I determined that we needed to intensify the remediation efforts for our athletes. The NCAA's decision to lower eligibility standards opened the floodgates for athletes who could not compete academically. I hired a licensed psychologist, Nicki Moore, primarily to assess the academic skills of our athletes and secondarily to provide counseling services. Soon she requested additional assistance, and more psychologists were hired. We added two reading specialists and a fleet of around twenty-five learning specialists to monitor athletes' progress on their coursework. The number of athletes diagnosed with learning disabilities rose significantly, along with the number of athletes who were at the level of functional illiteracy. Although the academic center had tutors and all the assistance a serious student could possibly need, our unit devoted significant effort and resources to basic remediation. We were teaching skills that these athletes should have acquired in elementary school.

For too many marginally prepared athletes, the concept of attaining a quality education at OU changed from ambivalence to overt resistance. Acquiring an improvement in literacy and study skills requires effort and time. For some, the commitment necessary to improve was too great. Often feeling embarrassed in the classroom, athletes tended to avoid attending classes, act out as class clowns, and fail to keep up with assignments or adequately prepare for exams. The pursuit of a college education became a nuisance. After all, these students felt that they were here to win on the football field or basketball court—not necessarily in the classroom. I asked myself if this resistance was unique to Oklahoma but soon discovered that my colleagues in major college athletic programs were experiencing the same shift in their athletes' behavior.

Thanks to the threat of NCAA punitive team measures in the Academic Performance Program, universities developed innovative efforts to maintain athletes' eligibility and even to graduate these at-risk athletes. Across the nation, the creation and expansion of large and lavish academic support centers continued to rise. These centers were typically housed apart from other athletic facilities and, as is tradition, were designed to impress prospective recruits. OU's most recent renovation cost millions and housed seven learning centers, advising offices, space for tutoring and learning specialists, and more.[3]

Most disturbing was the development of less stringent academic majors in which athletes could cluster to maintain their eligibility and ultimately graduate. Just before I arrived at Oklahoma in 1993, the university reviewed academic majors and dropped several that lacked academic rigor. Not surprisingly, those dropped (e.g., law enforcement, physical education, and general studies) were the most popular majors for athletes at that time. Between 1993 and 2007, high-risk athletes gravitated to sociology, communications, and criminology. These majors required a 2.0 grade point average (C average) to graduate and offered an abundance of elective credits.[4]

Stand-alone athletic academic centers became commonplace in the 1990s as a tool to lure recruits to campus and to put the importance of academics front and center. The phenomenon of building these centers was also fueled by the NCAA's Academic Performance Program, which put more of a focus on academic eligibility. Athletic academic facilities are some of the most opulent on campuses and can be as large as other academic buildings that serve larger numbers of students. Most are built with private donations. The growth of athletic academic centers also led to larger staff and monitoring systems to ensure athletes are able to remain eligible to compete. At Oklahoma, nearly 60 percent of athletes were "special admits," meaning they did not meet the university's admissions requirements.[a] The Sooners spent $2.9 million in 2007 helping athletes manage their schoolwork. On average, from 2007 to 2008, the athletics academic services office spent $6,213 per student on its 470 athletes—almost twice what the program spent ten years previously.[b]

To accommodate students known as "floaters" who wandered from major to major without making adequate progress, a general studies hybrid was created: multidisciplinary studies. The curricula included basic Oklahoma State Regents for Higher Education and OU general requirements but did not include more stringent academic requirements for a degree at any of the colleges at the university. The multidisciplinary studies major was designed to permit students more flexibility in developing their own degree programs; it rapidly became one of the most popular majors at the school. Multidisciplinary studies served a useful purpose for many academically competitive students who wished to design their own cross-disciplinary, academically challenging major. Marginal athletes, however, were attracted to the major because it offered a more direct path to graduation and, with abundant electives, made it easier to maintain eligibility. Multidisciplinary studies is not housed in a college at OU, for no faculty would approve such a major. Instead, it is administered in the College of Arts and Sciences and offered by the provost's office—a degree program atypical of others.

The NCAA's pressure to graduate more athletes led other universities to follow the same path. Agricultural leadership and development at Texas A&M, sports management and general studies at Michigan, and interdisciplinary studies and sociology at Oklahoma, all became popular majors for athletes to hide while maintaining their eligibility and even graduating with an "educational experience." What the NCAA advertises as an improved graduation rate is really an educational experience that vaguely resembles a college education. Faculty members on our campuses defend these majors for jocks while the value of our degrees declines.[5]

Athletes at Oklahoma who pursued the path of academic least resistance were practicing survival. They were trapped in a system that increasingly demanded their time through a semi-militaristic routine of physical training and practice. The most vulnerable had little option but to select their majors from a practical exclusion of more demanding curricula. Most coaches showed little patience or understanding for students with severe learning disabilities or deficiencies. When one of their high school recruits or current players was diagnosed with a learning disability, they were delighted to have an explanation of their previous poor performance. Coaches had no idea of the time and labor necessary to improve these students' academic performance. Where coaches viewed learning disabilities as a convenient truth that allowed them to explain the poor academic performance of their players, my staff and I saw a long, arduous challenge.

TEN

THE EPIPHANY

loved the creativity and flexibility that my role in athletics afforded me to build my support programs. I enjoyed the opportunities to positively affect the lives of athletes who wanted a better future. I loved my self-appointed role of teaching a new generation of future athletic administrators who might understand the ethical issues I struggled with regarding a profession in college athletics. However, the contradictions of working in the corrosive environment of greed in this athletic entertainment business had assuredly and gradually affected my outlook and my health. In July 2009, while recovering from back surgery, I suffered another heart attack. My recovery this time was not as rapid, and I felt personal anguish that continuing in athletics might eventually kill me.

The irony of the dubious and awkward marriage between big-time sports and American higher education was tearing at my sensibilities. I could not ignore the damage athletics had done to what I considered the finest higher education system in the world. Issues like the constant and valid complaints from faculty about the disruptions my athletes were causing in their classes, criticisms from scholars, and the public's growing cynicism about the NCAA continued to weigh heavily on my mind and strongly impacted my shifting attitudes toward college sports.

In June 2006, I received the National Association of Academic Advisors for Athletics (N4A) Lan Hewlett Award.[1] It is regarded as the most prestigious achievement in my profession and honors an academic support professional who serves as a mentor, researcher, and leader.

In 2009, the N4A selected me as president-elect, and my term began during the 2010–2011 academic year. By this time, I was outspoken in my criticism of what I considered the NCAA's failing academic reform efforts, particularly its new initial-eligibility standards. I authored and coauthored several commentaries about toughening NCAA standards. The N4A specifically asked me to champion the cause for stronger academic standards for athletes. I strongly believed that the NCAA's lowered standards hurt the possibilities for athletes to have meaningful educations, and I gladly accepted the responsibilities as a spokesperson for athletic and academic reform.

I spoke before the NCAA's Academic Cabinet to lobby for higher standards, but its leaders believed that the NCAA's efforts were making measurable strides in improving athlete graduation rates. As president of the N4A, I offered firsthand accounts of athletes admitted to Oklahoma who qualified under the NCAA to compete but could not read beyond an elementary school level. The Academic Cabinet, a group of mostly faculty athletics representatives (FARs) appointed by their presidents, dismissed these examples as anomalies. Most cabinet members sat in dead silence. I suspected that many of these distinguished faculty understood that similar academically underprepared athletes were on their campuses.[2]

These presidentially appointed FARs love the attention received by their administrations on campus, the trips to bowl games and away games, and the Nike team apparel and luggage. These faculty representatives received reduced teaching loads and significant salary increases for their work as the guardians of academic integrity in athletics. Many so enjoy the benefits associated with these positions that they remain in the role for decades. Their primary functions are to academically legitimize college athletics and to sanctify the NCAA's stated mission of integrating athletics into our universities' academic life. These are the very individuals who may turn a blind eye to the widespread scandals and cheating on their own campuses, and who can review and approve the admissions of woefully deficient student-athletes because the coach needs them to win games. This is not to say that all FARs are corrupt.

Many simply haven't realized the meaning of their roles. Some, like the late Lonnie Kliever from Southern Methodist University, are deeply committed to finding a means by which big-time college sports can coexist with academics in the university community—functioning like an extracurricular activity rather than a business enterprise.

In 2010, I gave a couple of presentations and a plenary speech at the Coalition on Intercollegiate Athletics (COIA) annual meeting. The COIA group was comprised of representatives from fifty-eight faculty senates interested in promoting athletic reform on their campuses.[3] My plenary speech focused on what I called "the original sin," which is the admission of athletes who are unprepared and unable to compete in the classroom for a meaningful education.[4] At this conference, I met faculty who shared my concerns about the academic compromises made in the college athletics entertainment industry and the damage it was causing to American higher education. Tom Palaima, a classics professor from the University of Texas, and Nathan Tublitz, a neurobiologist from the University of Oregon, were two outspoken professors I befriended. I also met Jon Ericson, the retired founder of The Drake Group (TDG), a faculty-based organization dedicated to reforming big-time college sports.[5] TDG is an association of individual faculty members rather than faculty senates. It was here that I was introduced to the core voice of academic opposition to college athletic commercialism. TDG met each spring at the College Sports Research Institute at the University of North Carolina, Chapel Hill.[6]

Although both the COIA and TDG were quite public, befriending and engaging them in conversation was considered an act of heresy for an athletic administrator. Later, I became well acquainted with other highly respected faculty conducting research and writing about intercollegiate athletics. Through my association with TDG, I met well-known authors, reform advocates, and speakers such as Dr. Allen Sack of the University of New Haven (an original member of TDG) and Dr. Ellen Staurowsky of Ithaca College (both original members of TDG); Sonny Vaccaro, an athletes rights advocate, former Nike basketball shoe marketing guru, and inventor of the famous Air Jordan shoe; Dr. Donna

Gerald Gurney presenting at the thirteenth Annual National Meeting of the Coalition on Intercollegiate Athletics at the NCAA National Office, 2016

Lopiano, a former director of women's athletics at the University of Texas and longtime advocate for women's sports expansion; Dr. David Ridpath, former longtime college athletic administrator and current professor at Ohio University; and Dr. Richard Southall, professor at the University of South Carolina and director of the College Sports Research Institute. I suspect their fascination with me developed from concepts I espoused through my op-ed pieces in *The Chronicle of Higher Education* and my pleas for higher academic standards in athletics. My position as a senior-level administrator in a major athletics program was also an oddity. Not surprisingly, my associations with athletic reformers from outside the athletic profession were noticed on my campus and in the athletic world.

My association and interaction with these reformers helped me and make sense of what I had experienced throughout my career. The professional readings I poured through and conversations I had with academic support colleagues, reporters, athletic administrators, and reformers helped me contextualize my personal experiences in athletics during the turbulent period in which I worked.

The Drake Group team (Donna Lopiano, Karl Isvoog, Lori Ulferts, Allen Sack, Mary Willingham, Gerald Gurney, David Hughes, and David Ridpath) in Washington, DC, to meet with members of Congress, 2018. *The Drake Group*

It became evident that the athletic administration and I would soon part ways. Athletic reform of intercollegiate athletics, teaching, research, and writing became my full-time passion and focus. I was asking questions that were uncomfortable for both my colleagues and me. Despite taking a critical view of big-time college sports, I remained devoted to the welfare of my athletes and my staff.

By the close of 2010, it was time to leave athletics. I had been in the same position in the University of Oklahoma Athletics Department for close to eighteen years and in the profession for thirty-one years. At Oklahoma, I observed the rapid escalation of the athletics arms race and the rising salaries in the coaching marketplace. There were great experiences at Oklahoma, including college championships in football, men's gymnastics, and baseball. Both men's and women's basketball went to the Final Four. Our football team participated in four national championship games. At Oklahoma, I worked with outstanding colleagues and a loyal and talented staff. I hired many graduate assistants who gained experience in the athletics department and moved on to great careers in higher education, athletics, and business.

One special graduate student, Carla Winters, served as my teaching and research assistant for six years. Without her assistance, I could not have managed all my administrative duties while teaching classes and researching the academic performance of athletes. Carla, who came from a family of academicians, developed excellent teaching and research skills and is the most promising young professional I know in intercollegiate athletics. In 2012, she completed her doctorate and then worked in the University of Oklahoma Athletics Department as a researcher and academic adviser. It was a privilege to be on her doctoral committee and to have played a part in her graduate education.

On November 10, 2010, my declining health, approaching retirement, and strong desire to continue teaching, writing, and researching, led me to negotiate with President Boren. Effective June 2011, I left my position in athletics to join the University of Oklahoma faculty. I was able to continue my connection with students while writing and researching the academic performance of athletes engaged in major college athletics. I felt that I had finally found the dream job I had hoped for after completing my doctoral program at Iowa State.

ELEVEN

THE ATHLETIC TRINITY

Presidents, Athletic Directors, and Coaches

Presidents run the college athletic entertainment industry. To fund higher education, presidents believe that activities like college football or basketball in enormous stadiums and arenas create a spectacle to amuse and satisfy fans. Wealthy trustees and major donors to universities live vicariously through the combat displayed by players and coaches for their schools. Similar to military generals or business managers, losing coaches are simply replaced. Winning coaches are handsomely rewarded. This scene has repeated since the first intercollegiate rowing contest in 1852.[1] There is very little, if any, connection between this spectacle and education. Presidents find value in portraying themselves as cheerleaders for college football and basketball. They do this because their governing boards demand it and because of the potential college sports has for positively influencing state legislators and potential donors.[2]

Big-time college athletics is a risky business, with great rewards accompanied by great risks. My former boss at the University of Maryland, William "Brit" Kirwan, later became chancellor emeritus of the University System of Maryland and was co-chair of the athletic reform–seeking Knight Commission on Intercollegiate Athletics.[3] Brit's co-chair was Southern Methodist University President R. Gerald Turner. Ironically, I had crossed paths with these men's institutions. Both Kirwan and Turner understand the terrible consequences of an out-of-control athletics system for higher education. Division I athletics departments average a $9 million plus debt[4] and draw considerable funding from the university's academic mission.[5] Much of the funding comes from student fees amid rapidly rising tuition and a troublesome jobs market.[6] Most experts find the rising costs of the athletics arms race and coaches' salaries unsustainable.[7] Yet our college leaders continue to buy into the "great magical myth of coaching" that says it's necessary to pay $5 million for coaches to bring winning teams to campus. This great illusion is perpetrated by the agents of grossly overpaid coaches who forget they work in an educational community with more important goals than winning football or basketball games. Now that the Bowl Championship Series playoffs have expanded even more into the College Football Playoff (CFP), millions more will be devoted to enhancing coaching salaries.

What I find most puzzling about college presidents' inability to exert fiscal and academic controls over athletics is that they are in control of the governance of the NCAA as well as the Bowl Championship Series (now CFP), which affect football revenue. College presidents serve on presidential oversight committees for both organizations, and have been miserable failures at controlling the damage done to their campuses. In a survey conducted by the Knight Commission, the vast majority of college presidents admit to being unable to make necessary changes on their campuses due to pressures exerted by governing boards and donors.[8] If that is the case, one would logically believe that college presidents could make the sweeping changes necessary while sitting on the critical governing boards of athletics. Instead, they become preoccupied with which athletics conference their school will join next and the size of the television broadcast contracts their conference will harvest.

By observing this vacuum in leadership, I conclude that most college presidents are satisfied with the status quo. They must view the debt incurred by their schools as an acceptable expense for what they gain. Rutgers University, as one example, plunged $26.8 million in debt in 2010, and nearly half of the athletic spending came from student fees, tuition, and other sources of nonathletic spending.[9] Although college presidents may see this pattern of excess in higher education as justifiable, athletics may not have the clear referendum to spend precious resources on lavish stadiums or outrageous salaries for coaches. Substantial angst and anger brew from faculty, students, government, and the public who do not share this enthusiasm.[10] College presidents participate in this university-sponsored entertainment because their boards demand this folly. If their teams have success, they share in the success. If their teams fail, they demand change.

The professional backgrounds of athletic directors have changed from former coaches to businessmen with marketing and development experience.[11] They are not particularly impressive as a group, although I have worked with several outstanding leaders. Many passed through the athletic system in earlier years, got their diplomas in general studies or a similar major, and never left. Internally, athletic directors are responsible for keeping their revenue-generating coaches satisfied, winning, and hiring staff that will keep the competition circus moving—all the while hoping their major sports will not run afoul of the NCAA rules, and the school will avoid penalties. Externally, their jobs are largely exploring new revenue streams to continue feeding the monster. Perhaps a wealthy donor will donate millions of dollars in exchange for naming a new facility. Athletic directors serve as coach enablers, generating whatever new project the coach insists is needed to help recruit or make a difference in a game. Indoor practice facilities, new strength and conditioning facilities, new training tables, and dining halls are always on the priority lists. At Oklahoma, a two-year-old museum dedicated to the legends of Oklahoma football was scrapped for a more impressive one. The same occurred with a locker room, equipment room, coaches offices, and meeting rooms—all to impress seventeen- and eighteen-year-old recruits. The football facilities at many colleges and universities are more opulent now than for any professional football franchise.[12]

The modern athletic director also spends a great deal of time developing strategic plans and mission statements that stress noble educational values and goals for leadership. The mission statement of the Oklahoma Athletics Department is "Inspiring Champions Today and Preparing Leaders for Tomorrow." This mission is in stark contrast to the daily rap sheets we read detailing the misdemeanors and felonies perpetrated by our privileged athletes. My observation of the college athletics leadership development for athletes is that the experience fails to develop character. Too often, the coaching role models presented to athletes value greed, cheating, and winning at any cost. Rules for athletes vary based on the players' individual contributions to winning. The future of the athletic director is inextricably linked to the winning output of their revenue sports coaches and keeping their celebrity coaches content.

Coaches maintain a mysterious aura of magic about them and convince fans, college presidents, and athletic directors that they can win perpetually. They live in a fraternity that adheres to a code of silence. The coaches' unwritten creed is to protect the head coach at all times, even if it means falling on their swords. Regardless of a coach's personal flaws, the program must be protected. Never admit to rule violations, even when the evidence is stacked against you. When your win-loss record improves, negotiate a new contract regardless of how many years remain on your existing contract. Reap as much as you can from your host university, for tomorrow you could be fired.

The coach's once-honorable role as an educator died in 1984 when the US Supreme Court ruled in favor of the plaintiffs in *NCAA v. Board of Regents of the University of Oklahoma*, finding the NCAA in violation of antitrust laws over television negotiation rights. The sudden influx of television revenues flowed into institutional coffers, making coaches progressively wealthier. The goals and values of coaches became a singular aim: to win more games. Teaching young men values to live by or developing their character through hardships and teamwork soon became a myth. Head coaches in all sports followed the example of football coaches and soon found willing sports agents to negotiate their contracts.

I left intercollegiate athletic administration at possibly its worst moment in history. The relevance of the NCAA and its mission of being an integral part of higher education and student-athlete development was in serious doubt. Any examination of intercollegiate athletics must begin by questioning whether the unsustainable costs of the spectacle are justifiable for American higher education, which was once the model for the world. Now, sadly, our students are finding a quality education elusive and unaffordable. We are admitting exceptional athletes who cannot compete in the classroom and justifying their admission by granting them degrees in unemployable general education. Meanwhile, the games go on, and our stadiums fill with fans lusting to feel like winners.

TWELVE

WINNERS AND LOSERS

At the vast majority of universities risking participation in Division I basketball and the football bowl subdivision, all but twenty-five manage to make a profit in a given year. Most institutions bear the brunt of an average of $9 million of debt, passed along to the students and parents who pay for their children's college tuition and student fees.[1] Taxpayers unwittingly also pay for this entertainment. Colleges enjoy tax-exempt status, and donors who purchase tickets or luxury suites write off 80 percent of the cost from their federal taxes.[2] These funds should have been paid to our federal government and represent tax advantages that the average non-sport attendee does not receive.

Large funds totaling billions are funneled through conferences and the NCAA to NCAA executives and conference commissioners. After the commissioners take their hefty slice, the remainder is channeled to athletic directors, who distribute the lion's share to revenue sport coaches. A relatively small portion of this bonanza directly or indirectly benefits the athletes. There is no end in sight for this gluttony and shameful mismanagement. Athletes' time is so limited that it is nearly impossible to receive a quality education that might challenge their academic potential. They typically settle for a degree they have been directed to study.

In the meantime, the NCAA public relations machine continues to promulgate the myth of amateurism and the image of happy young athletes skipping to class carrying backpacks. The top athletic administrators earn a comfortable living driving around town in new dealer cars and Nike polo shirts. The athletic director and head football and basketball coaches may have two dealer cars at their disposal, with perhaps free use of private jets to fly them away to exotic locations for vacations. The mentality they exhibit is not that of a state employee but that of a corporate CEO or rockstar.

Athletes have no guarantee of the funding they may need, after years of eligibility have expired, to return to the university to obtain the educational opportunities taken from them by their coaches. Further, athletes risk physical and psychological harm, such as the potential of brain injury or other serious lifelong injury or disease, from participating in athletics; all with no guarantee of the lifelong medical treatment they may need.[3]

Generally, there are no standards for the certification of coaches in the United States. Therefore, many coaches lack the training and credentials to practice coaching that prioritizes the well-being of athletes. Pressured to produce winning teams, coaches often transfer that pressure to their athletes who are expected to commit to year-round training—sacrificing study time and sleep to watch more film, lift more weights, increase repetitions, run more laps, ignore the pain of injuries, and push through exhaustion. This prevailing "more is better" culture among athletics programs demands that the athlete remain stoic and silent about the many ways in which the system takes its toll on physical and mental health.

Fearful of losing their scholarships, starting positions, or even the time and attention of their coaches, athletes often remain quiet when coaches mistreat them. When coaches physically or verbally abuse athletes, assistant coaches or athletic trainers who observe the abuse are also pressured (implicitly or explicitly) to remain quiet—fearful they may lose their jobs. The more successful a coach is, the more likely athletic administrators are to look the other way—attending games to cheer them on but seldom supervising, observing practice, or criticizing coach conduct.

When a parent or athlete exposes an abusive coach, when an athlete dies, or when multiple members of a team are hospitalized with rhabdomyolysis (a life-threatening but preventable overexertion syndrome), the institution typically circles the wagons to protect its brand by negotiating a settlement to avoid litigation or commissioning an investigation by a friendly third party who finds little to no wrong-doing. On occasion, the offending coach may be warned, reprimanded, or suspended for a number of games, whereas a lower-level staff member (seldom the winning coach) may be terminated. Those in the best positions to support the health and well-being of college athletes have little oversight to ensure that they do so, and no direct financial incentives to prioritize health and well-being over winning records.

Though well-intentioned, NCAA policies increasing access to higher education for economically disadvantaged student-athletes have created the possibility of essentially open admissions. This has resulted in the "special admission" of many academically underprepared student-athletes. Prospective high-school student-athletes can qualify for eligibility without correctly answering a single question on a standardized examination, and many admissions officers fear rampant grade inflation on the transcripts they review.

On August 3, 2020, US Senators Cory Booker, Richard Blumenthal, Christopher Murphy, Kirsten Gillibrand, Ron Wyden, Mazie Hirono, and Kamala Harris issued a "College Athletes Bill of Rights" statement that sought to advance justice and opportunity for college athletes and promised future legislation to realize their position.[a] On August 13, they were joined by Senators Bernie Sanders, Chris Van Hollen, and Brian Schatz. The Drake Group (TDG) applauded the initiative and urged Congress to give college athletes full outside employment and name, image, and likeness (NIL) rights.[b] TDG is a strong voice in the governance of college sports, comprehensive coverage for medical costs related to athletic injuries, protection from abusive coaches, mandated five-year athletic scholarships, and other academic protections to improve educational outcomes. On September 8, 2020, TDG proposed a College Athletes Rights and Protection Act (CARPA) to accomplish all of the promises made in the "College Athletes Bill of Rights" statement issued by US senators. Gerald Gurney and his TDG counterparts played a pivotal role in developing CARPA.

In order to remain eligible to compete, at-risk student-athletes are often caught in the twin pincers of underpreparedness and increased demands for academic performance. Once in college, these student-athletes often feel like impostors who do not belong among students far better prepared for the demands of college work. Although most student-athletes do well in their studies, the glaring exception is for those in men's basketball and football—the two "revenue sports" associated with almost all of the publicity, visibility, notoriety, and fraud in intercollegiate athletics. Is it any wonder such circumstances compound pressures on at-risk student-athletes and the athletic programs responsible for their academic eligibility to play?

The entire culture of big-time sports encourages academic misguidance and fraud. To limit the risk of NCAA penalties for unmet academic standards, universities engage in "creative" academic advising—clustering student-athletes into majors most likely to ensure their eligibility (regardless of their academic value to the student)—and sometimes engage in cheating, plagiarism, and other forms of academic fraud. College officials, beginning with coaches, engage in deception designed to exploit athletes' talents for entertainment and revenue-raising purposes, unconcerned about whether the student-athlete gains the broader benefits of higher education.

In addition to piling up debt, many college athletics programs are awash in academic scandal. Every time a student is admitted under essentially false premises, academic institutions give away a piece of their integrity, which is in direct opposition to the long-term well-being of academic institutions and higher education more broadly. The NCAA represents its own interests in these dynamics, the educational interests of academic institutions often go unrepresented.

Perhaps the biggest loser of all is American higher education, as our great universities continue to invest in an academically fraudulent, fiscally draining, and morally corrupt activity that draws from their main objective of advancing knowledge and preparing our youth for the important challenges we will face in our future. The rest of our world's universities refuse to admit students who do not academically earn a position in college. America insists on creating shameful exceptions for athletes. We would be wise to change the course of these policies before America loses its edge in higher education.

Given the complexities and competition the United States will be facing, the best course would be for universities to abandon the de facto professional college leagues of today and diminish the current madness of big-time college sports. Although our future begs for change, nothing short of collapse and catastrophe in higher education will significantly alter the course of greed and America's appetite to join the spectacle of big-time college sports.

THIRTEEN

THE PROSPECTS FOR CHANGE IN BIG-TIME COLLEGE SPORTS

The NCAA, college presidents, athletic directors, coaches associations, and television networks are linked inseparably in an industry designed to support their mutual interests. To expect any of these groups to relinquish strangleholds on the enterprise voluntarily is foolhardy. Any benefits to the well-being of the athletes or their roles as students are incidental asides to the primary goal of serving the economic well-being of masters. Even a massive scandal such as what we've seen at the University of Miami—where Nevin Shapiro allegedly provided millions of dollars in extra benefits to athletes, prostitutes for players and recruits, and abortions for the girlfriends of players—will not alter the course or popularity of the college entertainment spectacle. Not even the risk of scandal and the academic reputation of a prestigious school like the University of North Carolina at Chapel Hill—where courses were designed to maintain athletes' eligibility—will teach our institutions an ethics lesson.[1] The growing obsession, overindulgence, and scandals accompanying big-time college sports will likely continue on our campuses.

Reliance upon college presidents to take control of athletics seems foolish. No amount of scandal or degree of shame seems to spur their commitment to serious reform. There is little evidence that college presidents are individually willing or able to control the damage of athletics to their campuses nor collectively on the NCAA Board of Directors. Not since Robert Maynard Hutchins eliminated football at the University of Chicago in 1939 and pulled out of the Big Ten Conference has a college president stood up for integrity. Hutchins said, "A student can win twelve letters at a university without learning how to write one." I wonder how he would view American higher education today.

The only hope for corrective reform is a coalition between independent faculty and students interested in restoring affordable higher education. Faculty responsibility on campus is to safeguard academic integrity. It is under this premise that faculty should act to restore college courses and majors that offer a meaningful education to those participating in athletics. Whether faculty members choose to exercise their authority on campuses is another matter entirely. Past instances of faculty outrage and calls for reform of athletics have typically been short-lived. Faculty enthusiasm often wanes, then the responsibility passes to the provost or university administration as the semester gets underway and faculty begin teaching.

On the other hand, tenured and committed faculty can organize students who value their education and desire relief from rising tuition and fees. Strategies undertaken by a faculty and student coalition to reform athletics might begin with a focus on the "original sin" of

Robert Maynard Hutchins, president of the University of Chicago from 1929 to 1951, opposed the rampant commercialization of college football, which he said undermined the core values of higher learning. He was a strong advocate of academic integrity and avid defender of academic freedom and faculty's moral responsibility to be "truth tellers."[a] It was this stance that led Hutchins to pull the powerhouse University of Chicago out of the Big Ten Conference and deemphasize athletics at the elite institution in 1946. Before that, he moved resources away from athletics and downgraded the once-proud football program, which had Heisman Trophy winner Jay Berwanger, before shutting it down completely in 1939. UC stopped playing Big Ten basketball in 1944.[b] The Drake Group annually presents the Robert Maynard Hutchins Award to faculty or staff who take a courageous stand (often risking job security) to defend academic integrity at their institutions in response to institutional pressure related to the special treatment of athletes. Past winners include longtime reformers Dr. Bill Dowling, Dr. Harry Edwards, and Dr. Jon Ericson.

intercollegiate athletics: the special admission of vastly underqualified athletes. Students see these athletes in the classroom and resent them for taking up space and holding back the students there for education.

If faculty do nothing other than implement more stringent athletic admission policies and oversight, this action will have the greatest impact on campus athletic reform. Dedicated tenured faculty with data-based criteria must vigorously and regularly review the admissions of athletes. The admissions process for specially admitted athletes must resemble that of specially admitted students from the broader student body—ensuring that all students meet minimum academic competencies and can compete in the classroom. This will undoubtedly be unpopular and opposed by university presidents, administrations, athletic directors, and certain revenue-generating coaches. Still, nothing is more important for both the welfare of the athlete and the university. To take greater admission risk by enrolling athletes without basic learning skills puts tremendous pressure on the athlete and academic support staff. When faced with the possibility of losing a highly recruited prospect, faculty should consider the experience of the underprepared athletes and the possibility that another university or community college may be better suited for them. Schools should set standards most appropriate for their student body rather than the current minimal NCAA standards.

Faculty should insist that admissions reviews must be completed before offering athletic-related aid. Too often, a coach's premature offer of a scholarship to a prized recruit becomes an implied offer of admission. Today, it is quite commonplace to secure commitments from next year's class of recruits before the start of an academic year. Verbal commitments are often announced by prospects and published in the newspapers before any admissibility reviews.

The academic performance of the current student-athlete population should be carefully studied to determine the type of risk they represent for the institution. Faculty should provide unambiguous admissions guidance to the athletics department and coaches regarding the academic profiles desired for recruits. Some coaches take a more active role than others in encouraging team academic responsibility. Reward those coaches who have proven to be interested in the academic well-being of their student-athletes and who work in concert with the mission of your institutions by permitting greater admissions latitude. Do not reward coaches with poor graduation and persistence records of high-risk student-athletes.

There should be team limits for high-risk student-athletes. High-risk student-athletes should not exceed 30 percent of team composition. The strong academic culture of a team will lift the expectations of those student-athletes who are at risk. A poor team culture will undoubtedly result in poor performance and character issues.

Bonuses for coaches based on academic progress rate (APR) scores, grade point averages, or graduation rates are absurd. Students' academic performance on campus is everyone's primary responsibility and should not be reflected in an incentive just for coaches to get paid more.[2]

The organizational structure of academic support programs should be outside the athletics department and report to an academic unit on campus. Academic support programs for athletes ought to be financed by the athletic program academic entity to assist athletes' educational success. Though many organizational structures can work, I am convinced that this model affords the best opportunity for institutional control over athletics and is the best hope for relieving pressures on counselors and maintaining the athlete's best interests.[3]

NCAA academic reform must address the essential question of minimum admissions standards for athletes and the mastery of the most basic academic competencies. The NCAA's high school qualification standards for eligibility changes initiated in 2003 have failed our selective universities. It is clear to me that the open access and virtual open admissions standards created by the NCAA require an uncomfortable compromise that higher education should not willingly accept. NCAA academic reform must focus on academic preparedness, progress toward a meaningful degree, and graduation, not on points gained or lost for an obscure and faulty retention and athletic eligibility formula. I recommend that the NCAA return to the pre-2003 minimum standardized ACT and SAT scores of at least a 17 composite or an 820 combined verbal and math score. This is not because the test scores should be discriminating in nature and exclude potentially capable students; it is

Control of athlete academic support programs should not reside with nor be controlled by the athletics department due to obvious conflicts of interest. The drive to maintain athletes' eligibility for competition has led to numerous instances of academic fraud in college sports. These issues often begin with complicit academic support staff who may feel pressured to conform or fear losing their jobs if they do not comply. Many argue that unless athletic academic support staff report to an academic official, their focus may shift from helping to provide athletes with a valuable educational experience to merely ensuring their NCAA eligibility. This dynamic disproportionately affects Black athletes in revenue-generating sports like football and men's basketball. More than 50 percent of athletic academic support units are either controlled outside the athletics department or report to both the athletic and academic entities. The NCAA, along with organizations such as The Drake Group and the Coalition on Intercollegiate Athletics, recommends that athletic academic support units report to an academic entity as a best practice.[c]

because they are the only common standard measurements that assure minimal basic reading competencies. If better standardized measurements can be developed to counter the effects of high school grade inflation and underpreparedness, I would favor those.

Faculty should demand that the NCAA make all of its statistical data for initial eligibility available to the public. For too long, the APR formula design, justifications, and predictive values have been a well-kept secret. The scant information available to the public reads more like a public relations campaign. Further, the waiver requests and deliberations of the NCAA for penalty appeals should be made transparent for public scrutiny. The NCAA should explain its rationale for penalty relief. Perhaps a transparent process will restore public confidence in whom the NCAA sanctions or spares punishment.

Before institutions and coaches are penalized or rewarded by the NCAA, the APR measurement must become something that the public and university officials can trust as meaningful. Some serious discussion ought to take place about whether this metric should be abandoned along with the NCAA-manufactured graduation success rate. This graduation rate treats student-athletes as a special class of the student population and permits transfer adjustments for attrition, unlike any other student cohort. The federal graduation rate or other metrics that allow an athlete graduation comparison with the total student population is essential to the determination of athlete exploitation and any measurement of athlete success. The NCAA's preference for using its graduation success rate is a clever marketing shell game for its academic reform program.[4]

Faculty should encourage the NCAA to provide athletes with an incentive for graduating in four years by granting an exclusive extra year of athletic eligibility for those who graduate. By providing a fifth bonus year only for graduates, coaches may decide to recruit more capable students.

Students and faculty should insist that their campuses ban institutional subsidies of athletic programs using student fees, tuition waivers, and university operating budgets. Athletic operations must be self-sustaining, and spending must remain within their budgets. Adopting this strategy will change the face of college athletics as we know it because more than 90 percent of our universities in big-time football utilize subsidies and still operate in deficit spending. This strategy should force many institutions to retreat to lower levels and less expensive college competition. The end of athletic subsidies will reduce the excessive salary market for coaches and athletic directors, reduce student fee charges, and make quality education a bit more affordable for the public. Reducing athletic expenses will also mean more resources for the educational mission of our universities.[5]

Despite regular scandals in big-time sports, the prospects for change move slowly. The media has played an important role in countering the formidable NCAA propaganda machine. Athletic scandals have marred the credibility of the NCAA and its ability to govern and control wrongdoers. As evidenced by the Penn State University child molestation scandal, public figures and celebrity coaches cannot be relied upon to act conscionably.[6] Protecting the program and the coach's reputation can take precedence over protecting our children. Major conference commissioners are threatening to leave our current structure. They have realized that the NCAA's steadfast notion of amateurism is obsolete. Even if the role of the NCAA diminishes, I am uncertain that what will replace it will benefit the institution of higher education. Greed, revenue generation, and television coverage seem to outweigh the academic well-being of our students.

The career my father never understood or wanted for me has been difficult and rewarding. It has been my privilege to assist wonderful young people trying to carve out futures for themselves. I have supported the climb of economically disadvantaged athletes out of a cycle of poverty. College football and men's basketball programs have become training grounds for athletes aspiring to careers in professional sports. Unfortunately, the only connection between these sports and higher education is the name of the university the team borrows. While maintaining quasi-professional athletes in college entertainment, academic support systems keep the athletes on the field. The university is culpable for creating majors with suspect academic rigor—independent studies courses with little or no discernible educational requirements or value with professors who assign undeserved grades.

For the winners, the high-stakes game of college sports can yield a temporary flow of cash and excitement, like an intoxicating drug-induced rush. But the universities that participate in this high-stakes crapshoot must accept the debt and degradation of their integrity. Faculty and students can and must take back their universities.

America's universities in major college sports will be forced to move in one of two directions. Those currently awash in debt will reestablish education rather than entertainment as their first priority by scaling back the size and scale of their athletic programs, exercising budgetary control of their athletics department, and treating them like any other department. The salaries of coaches and athletic directors will resemble those of professors. Banning the use of student fees and institutional subsidies for college athletics will bring these programs back to fiscal sanity, and raising admissions standards will return the hope for integrity. Players might be a step slower and not as many will become professional players, but the appeal of the games will remain for their fans and alumni. Throngs of fans will continue watching and filling college stadiums on Saturday afternoons, but a significant portion of the revenues realized from television and apparel contracts will be dedicated to the university coffers rather than coaches and athletic administration. When the football game kicks off, the public will watch competitors who are there primarily for a college education. Before higher education leaders see the wisdom of these changes, scandals will continue, and the debt gap will grow for most universities involved in big-time sports. The schism between athletic spending and mounting debt will eventually threaten to bankrupt many universities with athletic programs participating in big-time sports.

A likely scenario for college athletics is that conference realignment will settle on four super-conferences of sixteen schools each. These sixty-four universities will opt to continue our current highly commercialized model. Athletes choosing to participate in this model will be offered a salary and the option to attend class if they wish. These super-conference schools will form their own regulatory association, and the structure of athletics will resemble professional franchises that use the names of universities.[7]

Expecting legislators to pass reform laws to restore values and integrity to higher education is unlikely. Too much pressure from the sport-crazed citizenry will maintain the current course. What will emerge is a choice by universities in super-conferences to engage in an authentic professional operation that is divorced from their academic functions. Standards for admissions will be the athletes' speed, agility, and strength rather than the pretense of academic achievement or aptitude. Our nation will have its super spectacles with fewer programs participating, but this quasi-professional model will more authentically represent college sports as separate from higher education.

FOURTEEN

OKLAHOMA HEISMAN WINNERS AND OTHER GREATS

have had the distinct pleasure of meeting five University of Oklahoma (OU) Heisman Trophy winners. The Heisman Trophy is awarded to the best college football player each year. Though I knew all of them, I worked closely with Steve Owens as my boss and guided Jason White and Sam Bradford as my students. I met the 1952 winner, Billy Vessels, on several occasions. He served on a search committee for an OU athletic director, and I was impressed with his gracious demeanor. Vessels played for Bud Wilkinson. Many players from the Bud Wilkinson era shared the same quiet graciousness. They seemed grateful for the opportunity to play for a great coach and appreciative of the education they received. Vessels played for the Sooners from 1950 to 1952 and passed away in 2001.

Steve Owens won the Heisman in 1969, the year I graduated from high school. He played running back for Chuck Fairbanks and was a tough, bruising football player. Steve is one of the kindest and most caring individuals I have met. He greets strangers with an instant smile and hugs them, and makes them feel like the most important people in the room. I am very proud to have maintained a close friendship with Steve. Although I suspect Steve would not have been interested in a long-term reign as athletic director at Oklahoma, he had all the skills to be a great one. People loved to be part of his team and would do any-thing to meet his expectations.

Billy Sims earned the Heisman in 1980. He played for Barry Switzer. Billy is publicly loud and brash. He would attend a number of athletic events, but often his interests appeared focused on the profit he could realize from the use of his celebrity rather than support for the football program. I am told that Billy is a genuine person, but I have mostly observed his entrepreneurial side.

Jason White was a great athlete who won the Heisman in 2003 despite two serious knee injuries. He is a courageous young man who is a small-town country boy from Tuttle, Oklahoma. I watched him mature over the years from a late-adolescent athlete to a mature graduate. Jason could not parlay his Heisman fame into a professional career but has been a successful businessman in Oklahoma under the tutelage of his mentor, Steve Owens.

The 2008 Heisman winner was Sam Bradford from Putnam City, Oklahoma. Bradford is Native American, a member of the Cherokee Nation. Over my career, I have worked with thousands of athletes. My favorite is Sam Bradford. Sam's intellectual capacity is boundless, and he was an exceptional student. Apart from his superior athletic talent, he cared deeply about his teammates and retains a fondness and generosity for his university. Sam has the quiet confidence of a winner. Despite his celebrity as a starting NFL quarterback, he is humble in all his dealings.

Gerald Gurney and Sam Bradford, 2009

Sam left for the NFL early. His father called me to work out a plan for the completion of his bachelor's degree in finance. After chatting with Sam's father, I couldn't help but tell him that if there was a Heisman Trophy for parenting, he and his wife should win it. They raised a great son, and I feel confident that he will accomplish greatness beyond his football career.

I've worked with many great athletes who became Oklahoma legends and trophy winners. The athletes who impressed me the most were those who quietly led by example and played selflessly. After his time at OU, Phil Loadholt went on to become the starting right tackle for the Minnesota Vikings. Phil is one of the largest human beings I have ever seen. In college, he stood six feet nine inches tall and 350 pounds. As one of my students, he worked particularly hard to honor a promise he made to his mother to graduate. I always appreciated Phil's willingness to sacrifice social time for academic goals. He is a quiet leader, one whose actions speak for him on the field and in the classroom, and I suspect it will serve him well throughout his life.

Phil Loadholt and Gerald Gurney, 2008

I most admired those OU football athletes who understood team-work and toughness. My high school football coach, Frank Gibson, told me to learn the difference between pain and injury. I still don't precisely understand that wisdom, but I got a sense of it watching a football player named Rocky Calmus. Rocky won the Butkus Award for best linebacker in the nation. As a student, he was painfully quiet. As a football player, he was tenacious and played with injuries that surely would have sidelined most athletes. A broken leg couldn't stop Rocky from playing. After playing on OU's championship team, he went on to play for the NFL Tennessee Titans.

Seth Littrell was another tough leader who played fullback on the 2000 championship team. A son of an OU football player, Seth could be counted on for short yardage in tough situations. He was dependable for making key blocks that protected quarterback Josh Heupel, or for creating opportunities for our running backs. Seth went on to become the offensive coordinator for the Indiana Hoosiers and the head coach for the North Texas football team. Both Seth and Rocky were solid students and even better people.

Another personal hero of mine was Nate Hybl, a quarterback for OU in 2001 and 2002. When Jason White sustained his knee injuries, Nate stepped in and was terrific. He excelled in the classroom and earned a degree in business from OU. He was also the 2003 Rose Bowl game MVP against the Washington State Cougars. Nate was a quiet leader who performed on the field and in the classroom.

Carl Pendleton was another quiet hero of mine. He played defensive tackle for the Sooners from 2004 to 2006. Carl and his younger brother Kierstan were raised by his mother in a single-parent home. When their mother became physically unable to raise them, Carl was given guardianship of his younger brother. Determined to carve out a better life for his brother, Carl raised him in Norman, supporting both of them with his meager athletic scholarship. He graduated with a degree in sociology and won numerous athletic honors. He then completed a master's in higher education while working in OU's Athletic Development Office. After graduating, Carl was offered a full-time position in Athletic Development at OU but declined the offer to enter the Norman Police

Academy. Carl went on to become a Norman police officer. Carl's life has been defined by his strength of character.

Another personal hero of mine arrived at OU in 1992—a wide receiver named Michael McDaniel. Michael came from John Marshall High School in Oklahoma City. He failed to qualify for competition out of high school and was required to sit out his first year. He was a very spiritual young man who became an ordained minister while in college. Michael worked very hard in college and graduated with a bachelor's in political science. He worked for me in the athletics department for a time and married a wonderful OU volleyball athlete named Kartina Sullivan. Michael later took a position in academic counseling at Oral Roberts University and became an assistant athletic director there until he took a full-time ministry position. At Oral Roberts, Michael earned his master's in public school administration. Kartina earned a doctorate in education from OU and went on to

Clay Bennett, Barry Switzer, Carl Pendleton, Kenny Mossman, Jake Sandefer, Joe Washington, Bob Stoops, and Gerald Gurney at the 2006 National Football Foundation and College Hall of Fame Banquet at the Waldorf Astoria in New York City

become an elementary school principal. She and Michael have often visited me with their three boys.

Many great female athletes crossed my path throughout my career. As a rule, women take much better advantage of athletic scholarship opportunities, often graduating before their eligibility is exhausted and even completing graduate programs before their five years of financial aid expire.

A young tennis player, Annette Bryntesson, came to OU on scholarship from Perth, Australia. Annette had a tough life. When she was fifteen years old, her father died suddenly of a heart attack. She was taken in by a tennis matron. Through Annette's initiative and grit, she earned a scholarship to come to the United States to study and play tennis. Our family virtually adopted her, and she became my daughter's big sister. She went on to be my graduate assistant in OU's Higher Education Administration master's program and learned the essentials of athletic academic advising. She became a senior academic adviser for the football team, then an assistant dean of students in a college at OU. I gave Annette away at her wedding. She makes me proud every day.

Gerald Gurney, Annette Bryntesson-Moran, and Craig Moran, 2006

Jackie Dubois is another courageous young athlete I've worked with. Jackie, a talented track athlete, suffered from cystic fibrosis—a deadly lung disease—since childhood. Jackie and her parents were told that she would not live past the age of fifteen. Instead of accepting that prognosis, Jackie turned to running as a means of staving off her illness. She never stopped running. Eventually, she became the captain of the cross-country team. Through her participation in cross-country running, Jackie has extended her life. She also excelled in her studies and graduated at the top of her class in meteorology, which is considered OU's most competitive major. She went on to complete her master's in meteorology and works as a professional meteorologist. While doing so, she married and now has two boys. Her husband, Adam Smith, a former graduate assistant of mine, went on to become an athletic director of a private high school in Dallas. Although their future is uncertain, I know they will face it with courage, conviction, and love for each other.

Another notable athlete and hero is Caton Hill, a player for Head Women's Basketball Coach Sherri Coale from 2000 to 2004. Caton earned a medical degree from OU and then served as a captain in the US Army, caring for our soldiers in combat. She served a tour in Afghanistan. Caton comes from a family of dedicated officers and understands commitment. She is exceptionally bright, witty, and plainspoken. Like the vast majority of Oklahoma's athletes in non-revenue-producing sports, she took advantage of her education and contributed to the academic fabric of the university.

Desiree Taylor was another exceptional Oklahoma women's basketball player and one of the brightest athletes I have worked with. She earned a bachelor's in chemical engineering from OU. Deciding she would rather teach, Desiree went to Dallas to teach science to inner-city youth. After several years, she returned to OU to earn an MBA before deciding her true calling was to be an academic adviser for athletes. I hired her immediately without hesitation. After several years working as an adviser for OU, Desiree moved to Dallas to work as an academic adviser for Southern Methodist University, then went on to start a tutoring business.

The athletes I have described here are all exceptional in their own right. I simply stepped aside and admired their work. I apologize for not recognizing countless other impressive young people whom I had the honor of serving. Approximately 10 percent of my time was spent developing programs for and nurturing the talents of academic achievers. I targeted the use of a large NCAA Student-Athlete Opportunity Fund[1] available to athletes through a portion of the NCAA's basketball tournament contracts with CBS for postgraduate educational opportunities. It enabled a multitude of students to attend graduate and professional schools with considerable financing. In addition to expanding our awards recognition for scholars, I worked with Dr. Chris Howard at the Honors College to develop challenging courses for exceptional athletes.

EPILOGUE

Mary Willingham

The day that Dr. Gerald Gurney (Gerry to me) phoned me for the first time is etched in my memory. I was in my office on campus at the University of North Carolina, having just gone public with a story about UNC's academic fraud. As you can imagine, answering my office phone was often unpleasant due to angry colleagues and hate and death threats from the public. Gerry's call was much different. He reached out to support me and to nominate me for the 2013 Drake Group Hutchins Award. The awards ceremony took place on the UNC campus at the Friday Center. At that time, Dr. Richard Southall was teaching at UNC, and his Sports Research Institute (now at the University of South Carolina) was hosting its annual conference. UNC administrators and my past colleagues in the athletics department attempted to stop the event and the research poster presentation that followed. The whirlwind of media attention that followed went on for more than a year. Throughout this period, my new friend Gerry checked in often to see how I was doing. From 2013 to 2015, Gerry and I frequently swapped stories over the phone and conducted joint interviews with CNN, HBO, and ESPN. We appeared together in documentaries and on shows like *Schooled: The Price of College Sports* (EPIX),[1] *Gaming the System* (HBO),[2] and *Dropping the Ball: The Shady Side of Big-Time College Sports* (SiriusXM and NPR).[3] We also participated in a panel organized by Senator Chris Murphy on Capitol Hill[4] and wrote articles for *Inside Higher Education*, *The Chronicle of Higher Education*, and *The News & Observer*. During this time, Gerry continued his work with The Drake Group (TDG), an organization founded in 1999 by Jon Ericson. TDG consists of professors dedicated to protecting academics in the face of big-time college sports. Over the past four decades, its mission has expanded to include educating policy leaders and ensuring the safety of college athletes. Gerry was part of TDG working group to "study college sports and formulate a vision of a new governing system for intercollegiate athletes."[5] Those of us with experience in the collegiate sports arena believe that change will continue, and Gerry certainly played a significant role in driving this change.

Personally, it was helpful that Gerry supported my claims about the low reading levels of special admit athletes, which UNC vehemently denied. Gerry, along with his colleagues and graduate students, had already been researching underprepared college athletes. Although he was working outside of the athletics department at the University of Oklahoma when we met, he still put himself in the way of critics in order to support me. I was, and remain, a much-hated whistleblower.

Ellen Staurowsky, Gerald Gurney, and Mary Willingham, "How Colleges Cheat Student-Athletes," panel hosted by Senator Chris Murphy, Washington, DC, July 25, 2019. *The Drake Group*

Gerry read and reviewed *Cheated*,[6] the book I coauthored with Professor Jay Smith, and was animated and excited about our success. He was especially thrilled with our review from Frank DeFord. This prompted me to ask Frank if Gerry could have his autograph, and Frank graciously obliged. Frank would later write a review for Gerry's coauthored book, *Unwinding Madness: What Went Wrong with College Sports and How to Fix It.*[7] I imagine Gerry and Frank laughing together at the hypocrisy surrounding the student-athlete. In 2015, Gerry kindly visited Chapel Hill again for our *Cheated* book launch party.

During the following eight years, I frequently spoke with and visited Gerry. He invited me to his classes at the University of Oklahoma to speak for several semesters, and his family hosted me at their lovely home. When I addressed his classes, Gerry always asked me, "Who at UNC knew?" As I rattled off the list—from academic advisers to deans, coaches, the admissions director, and a provost—he would laugh and exclaim, "Everyone knew!" He took a cynical delight in that part of the story. Gerry had the best laugh, and together we laughed about the utter ridiculousness of college sports fraud and the promise of a world-class education. "What a crock of BS," Gerry would often say.

We debated which of us disliked the NCAA machine more and which of us it hated more. I believe that together we shifted the conversation—allowing people to acknowledge that academic fraud was real and, more importantly, that it was deeply wrong. Gerry told me I was courageous. I explained that telling the truth wasn't difficult because, unlike lying, it doesn't require creating a story that you must maintain. The truth is simpler because it is always just that—the truth.

In cases of academic fraud—which Gerry and I both observed—we saw how the adults in these situations fail to uphold the higher education mission of providing students access to learning that fosters prosperity. I often say that college sports are just one more way that society keeps Black males uneducated and excluded from the economy, which seems to be a very intentional system of racism. Gerry and I both recognized that the biggest losers in Division I sports are the athletes who are promised a world-class education in exchange for their talents—a promise that is a lie, more often than not. For Gerry and for me, education is paramount. You may lose your health, money, friends, and sometimes family, but you will always have your education.

Gerry was proud of his education. He was also so proud of his family, his wife, Debra, and daughter, Rachel. He made a significant impact on so many people's lives, and his legacy of teaching and sharing his knowledge and experience will endure forever. Gerry kept in touch with many of his former students and had garnered a reputation of thoughtfulness and generosity among his graduate students in particular. When he invited me to visit his classes, he would assure me that I, too, would be treated like a star—and I certainly was. They just don't make people like Dr. Gerald Gurney anymore: brilliant, talented, kind, humble, and a bit salty. How lucky I was to have known him and to have called him both a friend and a colleague.

Though game days are spectacular, college sports offer a revealing snapshot of what is fundamentally wrong with our current culture. We seem to have lost sight of what is truly important. The business of college sports has taken precedence over education. As Gerry would put it, "They just want the money—big money."

Mary Willingham is coauthor of Cheated: The UNC Scandal, the Education of Athletes, and the Future of Big-Time College Sports.

NOTES

CHAPTER TWO

1. Brendan F. Quinn, "Johnny Orr (1926–2013), Who Built His Legacy at Michigan and Cemented It at Iowa State, Was More Than a Coach," *Mlive*, January 1, 2014, https://www.mlive.com/wolverines/2014/01/in_remembrance_johnny_orr_1926.html.

Johnny Orr, who passed away in 2013, was the former head men's basketball coach at the University of Michigan for twelve seasons and led them to the 1976 NCAA championship game against an undefeated Indiana Hoosier team coached by Bob Knight where they lost. He stunned the college basketball world when he left Michigan for more money at Iowa State University in 1980.

2. NCAA initial-eligibility standards for competition have gone through various iterations since the start of the NCAA in 1909. For the most part, up until the 2.0 rule in 1973, intercollegiate athletic eligibility was determined by the institutions. It was certainly open season on determinants for athletic eligibility by institutions, considering the stakes of keeping certain players on the field (Ridpath 2002; Staurowsky and Ridpath 2005; Waller 2003, 191). The NCAA attempted "to establish uniform eligibility requirements that would supersede those of member colleges and universities" in 1962 (Staurowsky and Ridpath 2005; Waller 2003, 193). The NCAA Executive Committee, a committee comprised of educators and administrators at NCAA member institutions, allocated funds to finance a study to examine whether academic success could be predicted for athletes based on their high school academic record and initial year of collegiate enrollment (Falla 1981, 145). The committee recommended developing an expectancy table to determine predictors for academic success in college. The table was based on high school grade point averages (GPAs) and scores achieved on one of the standardized entrance examinations, the American College Test (ACT) or the Scholastic Aptitude Test (SAT). In 1965, the NCAA Convention adopted the expectancy table, renaming it the "1.6 Rule" (Falla 1981). The 1.6 Rule was based on a relatively complex formula that attempted to predict an incoming student-athlete's ability to maintain a 1.6 GPA during his or her first year of college (Falla 1981; Waller 2003, 193). In effect, the 1.6 Rule meant that incoming freshmen, though not eligible to compete at the time, could not practice or even receive an athletic grant if they did not present an academic profile that predicted they would achieve a 1.6 GPA.

3. The 2.0 Rule addressed the issue of competition and athletic financial aid in an athlete's first year of enrollment but did not address lack of college preparatory

classes and standard institutional admissions, which still left the admissions process of athletes up to each institution. This standard would stay in place until the beginning of the next push for academic reform in intercollegiate athletics in 1984 (McMillen and Coggins 1992). The first suggestion to use a 2.0 grade point average (GPA) as a predictor of academic success in college for athletes was introduced at the 1973 NCAA Convention (Falla 1981). The 2.0 Rule abandoned standardized testing and required only that prospective student-athletes complete high school with a 2.0 GPA (Waller 2003). The 2.0 legislation superseded and replaced the 1.6 prediction table system by stating athletic grants-in-aid be limited to athletes who have graduated from high school with a minimum GPA of 2.0 for all work taken and certified officially on the high school transcript (Falla 1981). Despite the clarity of the 2.0 Rule post-1973 and its perceived improvement over the national 1.6 standard, there were still several ways that colleges and universities could circumvent this legislation, including what was still ultimately the individual institution's prerogative at the time to determine who was eligible, and who was not, to compete on the fields of play (Staurowsky and Ridpath 2005).

4. NCAA v. Board of Regents of University of Oklahoma, 468 U.S. 85 (1984). See https://supreme.justia.com/cases/federal/us/468/85/.

The biggest challenge to college sports being an integral part of education was the growth of television and other media in the latter half of the twentieth century. It is difficult to fathom today that, as recently as the mid-1980s, a person could watch only one college football game per weekend and potentially another regional game. For example, if Ohio State was playing Michigan in football—one of the greatest rivalries in college sports history—the game had to be selected by the NCAA for national television coverage or it would not be available for the general public to watch. The logic behind this was multipronged. There was a belief that television, despite the potential mass marketability, would dramatically and negatively affect the home-gate revenue of participants. However, the potential for television revenue drove several schools, most notably the University of Oklahoma and the University of Georgia, to challenge the NCAA's authority to control television broadcasts in the *NCAA v. Board of Regents* case, which went all the way to the US Supreme Court in 1984. The NCAA lost in a 5–4 decision that forever altered the landscape of intercollegiate athletics and moved the collegiate system even further from a primary focus on the academic mission for athletes. The NCAA also wanted desperately to control broadcasts and revenue, not just to protect the live gate, but also in an attempt to provide a level playing field among competitors. The fear was, if schools and conferences negotiated their own television and other media contracts, it would lead to a system of haves and have-nots, along with damaging the live gate. This could influence schools to have a "do whatever it takes" mentality to get star players and star teams on the field or court, often superseding academic standards in order to make more revenue via television and, by extension, corporate sponsorship rights (Byers 1995; Ridpath 2002, 2018). Although it can be argued that a system of haves and have-nots existed since the beginning of college sports, it is true that this decision opened up unprecedented amounts of revenue for some schools in the more high-profile conferences. This in some ways forced smaller schools to overspend and overextend in a desperate attempt to keep up with the major institutions, often trumping educational priorities in the name of athletic success or facing the prospect of dropping out of Division I football altogether.

5. *Ross v. Creighton University*, 740 F. Supp. 1319 (N.D. Ill. 1990). See https://law.justia.com/cases/federal/district-courts/FSupp/740/1319/1952227/.

a. *Ross v. Creighton University*, 740 F. Supp. 1319 (N.D. Ill. 1990).

b. David Ridpath, "NCAA Division I Student-Athlete Characteristics as Indicators of Academic Achievement and Graduation from College" (PhD diss., West Virginia University, 2002), https://researchrepository.wvu.edu/etd/2428/.; Ellen J. Staurowsky and B. David Ridpath, "The Case for Minimum 2.0 Standard for NCAA Division I Athletes." *Journal of Legal Aspects of Sport* 15 (2005): 113–38.

CHAPTER THREE

1. One of the best books that covers the sordid Southern Methodist University NCAA scandal is David Whitford's *A Payroll to Meet* (1989) published by the University of Nebraska Press. SMU, although academically elite with a Texas who's who of graduates with deep pockets, was still a relatively small private school that had trouble recruiting and keeping up with the big-time football universities in the old Southwestern Conference. Other schools in Texas were more than double the size of SMU, much more well known, and much more successful in football on the national stage. Under pressure to compete at the same level as Texas and Texas A&M, the SMU football program engaged in ethics, rules, and recruiting violations for a number of years—mostly regarding paying top recruits money and benefits. When SMU's corruption came to light, the NCAA handed out its most serious punishment in the history of college sports—the "death penalty"—which canceled the team's entire 1987 schedule. The school followed up by also canceling the 1988 season before restarting the program in 1989 at a much lower level of competition. The corruption did not end with what was an initial probation starting in 1985. Even during this initial two-year probation (SMU's third NCAA probation since 1981), the football program continued maintaining a huge slush fund that was used to pay players because certain returning players were promised payments. The NCAA said thirteen SMU players received illicit monthly payments totaling $61,000 while the school was on probation. Unbelievably Bill Clements, chairman of the SMU board and governor of Texas, knew all about the slush fund and opted to phase out the payments rather than stop them immediately for fear that angry

players who were promised money might go public and create still more problems for SMU. Clements and the athletic director, Bob Hitch, decided that the football program had "a payroll to meet" to pacify the promises made to the returning players even though payments to recruits had stopped.

2. "About FARs," NCAA, accessed February 15, 2024, https://www.ncaafara.org/copy-of-fara-leadership.

3. Gerald Gurney, Donna Lopiano, and Andrew Zimbalist, "How College Sports Lost Its Way I" and "How College Sports Lost Its Way II," chaps. 1 and 2 in *Unwinding Madness: What Went Wrong with College Sports and How to Fix It* (Washington, DC: Brookings Institute, 2017); B. David Ridpath, Gerald Gurney, and Donna Lopiano, "Presidents Choose to Enable Academic Fraud in Athletics," *Journal of NCAA Compliance*, July–August 2019, 3–6; Gerald Gurney, Lisa Rubin, Sarah Stokowski, and B. David Ridpath, "The Original Sin of College Sports: College Presidents' Ineffectual Use of Special Admissions," *Journal of NCAA Compliance*, May–June 2020, https://tigerprints.clemson.edu/cgi/viewcontent.cgi?article=1017&context=ed_org_ldrshp_pub.

4. Jay M. Smith and Mary Willingham, *Cheated: The UNC Scandal, the Education of Athletes, and the Future of Big-Time College Sports* (University of Nebraska Press, 2019).

5. David Whitford, *A Payroll to Meet: A Story of Greed, Corruption, and Football at SMU* (New York: Macmillan, 1989).

6. Whitford, *A Payroll to Meet*.

7. "Scandal as Big as All Texas: Cheating among the State's Football Recruiters Reaches Even to Governor's Mansion," *Los Angeles Times*, March 12, 2019, www.latimes.com/archives/la-xpm-1987-03-08-sp-13578-story.html; Whitford, *A Payroll to Meet*.

8. B. David Ridpath, Mark Nagel, and Richard Southall, "New Rules for a New Ballgame: Legislative and Judicial Rationales for Revamping the NCAA's Enforcement Process," *Entertainment and Sports Law Journal: Symposium Issue on College Sports and the Law.* 6 (2008): 1.

9. "Scandal as Big as All Texas."

10. Dennis Dodd, "30 Years Later: The Legacy of SMU's Death Penalty and Six Teams Nearly Hit with One," CBS Sports, February 22, 2017, https://www.cbssports.com/college-football/news/30-years-later-the-legacy-of-smus-death-penalty-and-six-teams-nearly-hit-with-one/.

11. B. David. Ridpath, "NCAA Division I Student-Athlete Characteristics as Indicators of Academic Achievement and Graduation from College" (PhD diss., West Virginia University, 2002), https://researchrepository.wvu.edu/etd/2428/.; B. David Ridpath, Mark Nagel, and Richard Southall, "New Rules for a New Ballgame: Legislative and Judicial Rationales for Revamping the NCAA's Enforcement Process," *Entertainment and Sports Law Journal: Symposium Issue on College Sports and the Law* 6 (2008): 1.

12. Ridpath, "NCAA Division I Student-Athlete Characteristics as Indicators of Academic Achievement and Graduation from College"; Gary A. Sailes, "The Case against NCAA Proposition 48," in *African Americans in Sports* (New York: Routledge, 2017), 133–44; Ellen J. Staurowsky and B. David Ridpath, "The Case for Minimum 2.0 Standard for NCAA Division I Athletes," *Journal of Legal Aspects of Sport* 15 (2005): 113–38.

13. Ridpath, "NCAA Division I Student-Athlete Characteristics as Indicators of Academic Achievement and Graduation from College"; "NCAA Graduation Rates: A Quarter-Century of Tracking Academic Success," NCAA, October 28, 2014, https://www.ncaa.org/sports/2014/10/28/ncaa-graduation-rates-a-quarter -century-of-tracking-academic-success.aspx.

In 1983, Proposition 48 was the first major attempt (other than a general high school grade point average [GPA] requirement) for a national initial-eligibility standard to combat widespread academic deficiencies in intercollegiate athletics. The rule initially required a minimum 2.0 high school GPA in eleven core academic courses and a minimum SAT or ACT score (700 and 15, respectively) to be eligible to compete in athletics as a college freshman. Proposition 48 was slated to begin in 1986 and was not without controversy. Tying competitive athletic ability to high school college preparatory class GPA and a corresponding score on the ACT or SAT was debated at the highest levels of the NCAA, government, and the courts—the main issue being that these standards would adversely affect those from lower socioeconomic classes and potentially substandard educational backgrounds, specifically for African American athletes. There is also widespread evidence that standardized college admissions tests are culturally biased and that test-score standards unfairly affect racial/ethnic minority student-athletes and student-athletes from disadvantaged backgrounds. Due to protests, court cases, and questions from elected officials, Proposition 48 underwent several proposed changes over the next several years in an effort to boost graduation rates and academic primacy while acknowledging the justifiable issues many had with the rule. In 1992, Division I institutions adopted Proposal 16, which modified Proposition 48 standards by establishing a "sliding scale" of test scores and high school GPAs that do not go below a 700 SAT or 17 ACT and a 2.0 GPA. Proposition 16 also established a partial qualifier standard in Division I (now called an "academic redshirt"), wherein an athlete who met either the test score or GPA standard could still receive an athletic scholarship and practice but not compete during the initial year of enrollment.

CHAPTER FOUR

1. David Nakamura and Mark Asher, "10 Years Later, Bias's Death Still Resonates," *Washington Post*, June 19, 1996, https://www.washingtonpost.com/

wp-srv/sports/longterm/memories/bias/launch/bias19.htm; Jack McCallum, "The Cruelest Thing Ever," *Sports Illustrated*, June 30, 1986, https://vault.si.com/vault/1986/06/30/the-cruelest-thing-ever.

2. Nakamura and Asher, "10 Years Later, Bias's Death Still Resonates."

3. Rick Telander, "You Reap What You Sow," *Sports Illustrated*, February 27, 1989, https://vault.si.com/vault/1989/02/27/you-reap-what-you-sow-oklahoma-has-paid-the-price-for-the-anything-goes-attitude-that-coach-barry-switzer-has-allowed-to-take-root.

The University of Oklahoma football scandal ended the Barry Switzer coaching dynasty with the Sooners, and the football program was put on a three-year NCAA probation in 1986. Violations included offering cash and cars to recruits and airline tickets to players. The NCAA Committee on Infractions stated that the university failed to exercise appropriate institutional control over the football program. During the probation, star quarterback Charles Thompson was charged with selling cocaine to an undercover officer. Other Oklahoma football players were accused of gang rape and firing weapons in the football dorm, to name a few offenses. Under pressure, Switzer resigned as head football coach on June 19, 1989. He would never coach college football again, but he did have later success in the NFL leading the Dallas Cowboys to the Super Bowl and winning in 1996.

4. "Bylaw, Article 19 Infractions Program," NCAA, accessed February 15, 2024, https://web3.ncaa.org/lsdbi/search/bylawView?id=11781.

A "show-cause order" under NCAA bylaw 19.02.3 requires a member institution to demonstrate to the satisfaction of the Committee on Infractions why it should not be subject to a penalty (or additional penalty) for not taking appropriate disciplinary or corrective action with regard to violation of NCAA bylaws. Contrary to popular belief, this does not automatically mean that a coach or involved individual must be fired; it simply means that if the institution or another institution hires someone under a show-cause order, the institution could be subject to further penalties by the NCAA. Therefore, most who are under a show-cause order find it very difficult to keep their jobs or be hired in a similar position, at least for a number of years.

5. B. Porto, G. Gurney, D. Lopiano, D. B. Ridpath, A. Sack, M. Willingham, and A. Zimbalist, "The Drake Group Position Statement: Fixing the Dysfunctional NCAA Enforcement System," April 7, 2015, https://www.thedrakegroup.org/wp-content/uploads/2019/06/tdg-position-fair-ncaa-enforcement.pdf.

6. B. David Ridpath, Mark Nagel, and Richard Southall, "New Rules for a New Ballgame: Legislative and Judicial Rationales for Revamping the NCAA's Enforcement Process," *Entertainment and Sports Law Journal: Symposium Issue on College Sports and the Law* 6 (2008): 1.

7. "Enforcement: Division I Internal Operating Procedures," NCAA, 2023, https://ncaaorg.s3.amazonaws.com/enforcement/d1/D1ENF_EnforcementIOPs.pdf.

8. Amy Goldstein, "Wade Quits after Rocky Three-Year Stint as Coach," *Washington Post*, May 13, 1989, https://www.washingtonpost.com/wp-srv/sports /longterm/memories/bias/launch/wadeq.htm.

NCAA investigators concluded that Wade provided improper benefits to enrolled Maryland basketball players including rides to class, misstatements to NCAA investigators, frequent flyer bonus points from airline tickets purchased by the athletics department, and occasional small cash payments.

9. Gerald Gurney, Donna Lopiano, and Andrew Zimbalist, "Academic Integrity," chap. 3 in *Unwinding Madness: What Went Wrong with College Sports and How to Fix It* (Washington, DC: Brookings Institute, 2017); Tom McMillen and Paul Coggins, *Out of Bounds: How the American Sports Establishment Is Being Driven by Greed and Hypocrisy—and What Needs to Be Done about It* (New York: Simon and Schuster, 1992); Gerald Gurney, Woodrow Eckard, and Richard Southall, "The Hoax of NCAA Graduation Rates," *Sports Litigation Alert*, December 22, 2017, https://sportslitigationalert.com/the-hoax-of-ncaa-graduation-rates/; "Graduation Rates," NCAA, 2013, https://www.ncaa.org/sports/2013/11/19/graduation-rates .aspx; Student Right-to-Know and Campus Security Act, H.R.1454, 101st Cong. (1990), https://www.congress.gov/bill/101st-congress/house-bill/1454/text?s=1&r =14&q=%7B%22search%22%3A%22sex%22%7D.

10. Gurney, Eckard, and Southall, "The Hoax of NCAA Graduation Rates"; Gurney, Lopiano, and Zimbalist, "Academic Integrity"; Allen Sack and Gerald Gurney, "The NCAA's Miraculous Graduation Rate! It Is Correct to Recognize Transfers Who Graduate, but the Flawed Formula Needs to Be Revisited," *Sports Business Journal*, May 6, 2019, https://www.sportsbusinessjournal.com/Journal /Issues/2019/05/06/Opinion/SackGurney.aspx.

---

a. Student Right-to-Know and Campus Security Act, Pub. L. No. 101-542, 104 Stat. 2381 (1990).

CHAPTER FIVE

1. Jake New, "Attendance Monitoring Programs Common in College Athletics," *Inside Higher Ed*, June 23, 2015, https://www.insidehighered.com /news/2015/06/24/attendance-monitoring-programs-common-college-athletics.

2. Gerald S. Gurney, "Toughen NCAA Standards for Freshmen," *Inside Higher Ed*, February 6, 2011, https://www.insidehighered.com/views/2011/02/07/toughen -ncaa-standards-freshmen; New, "Attendance Monitoring Programs Common in College Athletics."

3. Joe Castiglione came to Oklahoma in 1998 after a successful five-year stint as the athletic director at the University of Missouri. He has been the athletic director

at the University of Oklahoma for almost three decades and was instrumental in bringing the athletics department out of debt to a model of fiscal sustainability.

———————

a. "For Faculty Who Have Student-Athletes in Class," University of North Carolina at Chapel Hill, accessed February 15, 2024, https://aspsa.unc.edu/for-faculty-who-have-student-athletes-in-class.

b. Jake New, "Attendance Monitoring Programs Common in College Athletics," *Inside Higher Ed*, June 23, 2015, https://www.insidehighered.com/news/2015/06/24/attendance-monitoring-programs-common-college-athletics.

c. Joy L. Gaston-Gayles, "Advising Student Athletes: An Examination of Academic Support Programs with High Graduation Rates," *NACADA Journal* 23, nos. 1–2 (2003): 50–57.

d. John R. Gerdy, *The Successful College Athletic Program: The New Standard* (Oryx Press, 1997).

e. Gaston-Gayles, "Advising Student Athletes."

CHAPTER SIX

1. Kirby Hocutt not only served in different athletic administrative roles at Kansas State, he also played football from 1991 to 1995 under Bill Snyder and knew Stoops well. Hocutt and Van De Velde both went on to become successful athletic directors at other Division I schools.

2. Gilbert M. Gaul, *Billion-Dollar Ball: A Journey through the Big-Money Culture of College Football* (Penguin, 2015); Gerald Gurney and Mary Willingham, "Academic Fraud, Athletes and Faculty Responsibility," *Inside Higher Ed*, July 17, 2014, https://www.insidehighered.com/views/2014/07/18/professors-must-take-academic-fraud-among-athletes-more-seriously-essay; Matt R. Huml, N. David Pifer, Caitlin Towle, and Cheryl Rode, "Do Facilities Really Matter in Recruiting?" Athletic Director U., 2018, https://athleticdirectoru.com/articles/do-facilities-matter-recruiting/; Eric Kelderman, "Who Should Oversee Athletes' Academic Progress?" *The Chronicle of Higher Education*, January 28, 2018, https://www.chronicle.com/article/who-should-oversee-athletes-academic-progress/.

3. *Cureton v. National Collegiate Athletic Association*, 37 F. Supp. 2d 687 (E.D. Pa. 1999). See https://casetext.com/case/cureton-v-national-collegiate-athletic-assn.

4. *Cureton v. National Collegiate Athletic Association*, 37 F. Supp. 2d 687.

5. Heupel was a lightly recruited quarterback out of high school and ended up at Weber State University in Ogden, Utah, for two years after being redshirted due to an injury. He had challenges cracking the starting lineup at Weber State, finding himself behind former UCLA quarterback Steve Buck and former University of Pacific quarterback John Fassel (whose dad, Jim, was the head coach of the New

York Giants at the time). Heupel did start two games at Weber State but chose to transfer to Snow Junior College in Ephraim, Utah, in 1998 for a year to try to get into another Division I program. It was at Snow where he was discovered by Leach and showed up in Norman, Oklahoma, where he quarterbacked the Sooners for two years, became a Heisman Trophy finalist, and led Oklahoma to the national championship in 2000.

6. Eric Christianson and Hollie Geren, "NCAA Launches Latest Public Service Announcements, Introduces New Student-Focused Website," NCAA news release, March 13, 2007, http://fs.ncaa.org/Docs/PressArchive/2007/Announcements/NCAA%2BLaunches%2BLatest%2BPublic%2BService%2BAnnouncements%2BIntroduces%2BNew%2BStudent-Focused%2BWebsite.html.

In 2007, the NCAA pushed back against the narrative that it lacked academic primacy by enacting a new public relations slogan, "There are over 380,000 student athletes, and most of us go pro in something other than sports." The intent of the campaign was to demonstrate that academics matter and there is an effective balance between academics and athletics in NCAA-sponsored sports.

---

a. Eric Kelderman, "Who Should Oversee Athletes' Academic Progress?" *The Chronicle of Higher Education*, January 28, 2018, https://www.chronicle.com/article/who-should-oversee-athletes-academic-progress/.

CHAPTER SEVEN

1. The escalating arms race of exploding coaches' salaries and opulent athletic facilities is an issue in higher education overall and especially acute in athletics, as many believe that successful athletic programs have an almost guaranteed effect on application and enrollment yield—though the research is mixed and these claims are largely unproven (See Frank, "New Study Debunks Link among Winning College Athletic Programs and Increases in Donations and Quality of Applicants"; Gurney, Lopiano, and Zimbalist, *Unwinding Madness: What Went Wrong with College Sports and How to Fix It*; Hoover, "Oklahoma in the Early Phases of Building a New $175 Million Football Facility"; Litan, Orszag, and Orszag, "The Empirical Effects of Collegiate Athletics: An Interim Report"). The college (sports) arms race has become a competition to see who can provide a better, grander college experience in the name of attracting students and hopefully increasing institutional prestige, school pride, overall rankings, student selectivity, and ultimately more profits. However, as Frank notes, these upgrades far from guarantee success and can actually have negative repercussions for institutions ("New Study Debunks Link"). Since the NCAA is classified as an educational nonprofit and the labor force (college athletes) does not get paid, the growing pot of money from television and marketing rights

(at least for the major athletic institutions) essentially has to go somewhere, and it has mostly gone into staff expansion, salaries, and facilities (Hoover, "Oklahoma in the Early Phases").

2. Cornrich's website states, "For over 25 years, Neil Cornrich and NC Sports has been a leader in managing the careers of professional athletes and coaches" (www.neilcornrich.com). Cornrich was also the agent for other coaches, including former New England Patriots head coach and multiple Super Bowl winner, Bill Belichick.

3. Michael Florek, "A Breakdown of All the Big Bonuses Big 12, SEC Football Coaches Received this Season," *Dallas Morning News*, January 23, 2016, https://www.dallasnews.com/sports/2016/01/23/a-breakdown-of-all-the-big-bo nuses-big-12-sec-football-coaches-received-this-season/.

Academic bonuses became a popular augmentation to coach salary and benefit packages after graduation rate information was mandated to be made public. In Stoops's case, he had $333,000 worth of incentive bonuses in his contract in 2016: $200,000 of the incentives were for winning games, coach of the year, and conference and national championships; $133,000 of the bonus money was solely for academic-based incentives such as team GPA and graduation rates (Florek, "A Breakdown of All the Big Bonuses").

4. Richard Johnson, "College Football's Newest Coaches Have Some Interesting Incentives and Clauses in Their Contracts," *Sports Illustrated*, June 22, 2023, https://www.si.com/college/2023/06/22/coach-contracts-incentives-clauses.

5. Gerald Gurney and Mary Willingham, "Academic Fraud, Athletes and Faculty Responsibility," *Inside Higher Ed*, July 17, 2014, https://www.insidehigh ered.com/views/2014/07/18/professors-must-take-academic-fraud-among-ath letes-more-seriously-essay; Gilbert M. Gaul, *Billion-Dollar Ball: A Journey through the Big-Money Culture of College Football* (Penguin, 2015); Gurney, Lopiano, and Zimbalist, "Academic Integrity," in *Unwinding Madness*; Matt R. Huml, N. David Pifer, Caitlin Towle, and Cheryl Rode, "Do Facilities Really Matter in Recruiting?" Athletic Director U., 2018, https://athleticdirectoru.com/articles/do-facilities-mat ter-recruiting/; Eric Kelderman, "Who Should Oversee Athletes' Academic Progress?" *The Chronicle of Higher Education*, January 28, 2018, https://www.chron icle.com/article/who-should-oversee-athletes-academic-progress/.

6. The "sliding scale" for initial eligibility that Myles Brand championed no longer exists, as the SAT and ACT are no longer required for initial eligibility even if they are required by an institution. Many institutions and the NCAA in 2023 moved more toward high school GPA and performance in core academic classes as the main eligibility and admission benchmarks (NCSA College Recruiting 2024). The sliding scale that existed before 2023 was put in place to expand opportunities for athletes who may have high GPAs but do not test as well (along with removing inherent cultural bias issues) or vice versa (*NCAA Eligibility Center Quick Reference Guide*). As mentioned in Thamel and Duff's 2005 article, the sliding scale made it

much easier to manipulate standards and resulted in many academically underprepared college athletes getting into school.

7. Pete Thamel and Duff Wilson, "Poor Grades Aside, Athletes Get into College on a $399 Diploma," *New York Times*, November 27, 2005, https://www.nytimes.com/2005/11/27/sports/ncaafootball/poor-grades-aside-athletes-get-into-college-on-a-399.html.

8. Thamel and Wilson, "Poor Grades Aside."

9. G. Gurney, E. Lopiano, D. Snyder, M. Willingham, J. Meyer, B. Porto, D. B. Ridpath, A. Sack, and A. Zimbalist, "The Drake Group Education Fund Position Statement: Why the NCAA Academic Progress Rate (APR) and Graduation Success Rate (GSR) Should Be Abandoned and Replaced with More Effective Academic Metrics," 2015, https://thedrakegroupeducationfund.org/2015/06/07/drake-group-questions-ncaa-academic-metrics/; Gerald S. Gurney and Richard M. Southall, "College Sports' Bait and Switch," *ESPN*, August 9, 2012, https://www.espn.com/college-sports/story/_/id/8248046/college-sports-programs-find-multitude-ways-game-ncaa-apr; Gerald Gurney and Richard Southall, "NCAA Reform Gone Wrong," *Inside Higher Ed*, February 13, 2013, https://www.insidehighered.com/views/2013/02/14/ncaa-academic-reform-has-hurt-higher-eds-integrity-essay.

The NCAA academic progress rate (APR) was devised to measure team performance at maintaining athlete eligibility and retention. Minimum team performance thresholds were devised to roughly equate to a 50 percent federal graduation rate. Teams scoring below .925 on their eligibility and retention scale would be punished through loss of financial aid, and those scoring below .900 would be cited for more serious loss of scholarships, postseason bans, and potentially restricted NCAA membership. The NCAA also created its own graduation success rate, adjusting for the transfer pattern of athletes, which it felt was a better measurement of college athlete graduation. The NCAA academic reform measures in 2003 became Myles Brand's presidential cornerstone (Brand died in 2009). Brand marshaled support for academic reform by championing access to higher education for more minority athletes who might succeed in college. He vowed to also punish institutions, teams, and coaches who habitually ran off players and underperformed academically. Brand said when the APR was unveiled, "for the first time, the NCAA is holding teams and institutions accountable for the academic progress and success of their student-athletes. The goal of the academic reform package is to reinforce good behavior. The new reforms are tough but fair." Just a year later, he declared that the NCAA academic reform "is becoming one of our greatest success stories." However, the facts did not support this statement. Gains for minorities were minimal. Some schools were getting high APR scores, but many scandals showed those scores were primarily through manipulation and outright fraud (Smith and Willingham, *Cheated*; Thamel, "Top Grades and No Class Time for Auburn Players."). The APR program was criticized by the media and professionals in athletic academic counseling who speculated, largely correctly, that the changes would be a catalyst for large-scale cheating. The stakes to recruit and keep elite athletes in football and basketball have continued to grow. Coaches, institutional staff, and even faculty have employed clever methods to get athletes admitted and stay academically eligible to play—using the APR as an easy path to get there ("Division I Academic Progress Rate [APR]").

10. Gurney, Lopiano, Snyder, Willingham, Meyer, Porto, Ridpath, Sack, and Zimbalist, "The Drake Group Education Fund Position Statement."

11. Gurney, Lopiano, Snyder, Willingham, Meyer, Porto, Ridpath, Sack, and Zimbalist, "The Drake Group Education Fund Position Statement."

12. Gurney, Lopiano, and Zimbalist, "Academic Integrity," in *Unwinding Madness*; Gurney, Lopiano, Snyder, Willingham, Meyer, Porto, Ridpath, Sack, and Zimbalist, "The Drake Group Education Fund Position Statement"; Matthew R. Salzwedel and Jon Ericson, "Cleaning Up Buckley: How the Family Educational Rights and Privacy Act Shields Academic Corruption in College Athletics," *Wisconsin Law Review* (2003): 1053, https://heinonline.org/HOL/LandingPage?handle=hein.journals/wlr2003&div=41&id=&page=.

13. Salzwedel and Ericson, "Cleaning Up Buckley"; Frank G. Splitt, "The Student-Athlete: An NCAA False Claim?" The Drake Group Education Fund, 2019, https://www.thedrakegroupeducationfund.org/wp-content/uploads/2019/06/splitt_the_student_athlete.pdf.

14. Gurney, Lopiano, and Zimbalist, "Academic Integrity," in *Unwinding Madness*; Peter Jacobs, "Here's the Insane Amount of Time Student-Athletes Spend on Practice," *Business Insider*, January 27, 2015, https://www.businessinsider.com/college-student-athletes-spend-40-hours-a-week-practicing-2015-1; Brad Wolverton, "College Football Players Spend 44.8 Hours a Week on Their Sport, NCAA Survey Finds," *The Chronicle of Higher Education*, January 14, 2008, https://www.chronicle.com/article/college-football-players-spend-44-8-hours-a-week-on-their-sport-ncaa-survey-finds-395/.

NCAA Bylaw 17 limits mandatory practice and playing time, defined as countable athletically related activities, to twenty hours a week during the playing season. This does not include time spent on activities such as traveling to games, rehabilitating an injury, or so-called voluntary practices. Specifically, NCAA Bylaw 17.1.7.1, Daily and Weekly Hour Limitations—Playing Season, states, "A student-athlete's participation in countable athletically related activities shall be limited to a maximum of four hours per day and twenty hours per week." However, many exceptions exist that are listed in the bylaw and add to the twenty hours exponentially. College athletes are permitted to spend their free time however they like, and many athletes use it to practice or train on their own to get better and/or increase professional playing prospects ("Bylaws, Article 17 Playing and Practice Seasons").

15. Gerald Gurney, Lisa Rubin, Sarah Stokowski, and B. David Ridpath, "The Original Sin of College Sports: College Presidents' Ineffectual Use of Special

Admissions," *Journal of NCAA Compliance*, May–June 2020, https://tigerprints. clemson.edu/cgi/viewcontent.cgi?article=1017&context=ed_org_ldrshp_pub; Gerald S. Gurney, David Tan, and Carla Winters, "Specially Admitted Student-Athletes: Their Academic Performance, Persistence, and Graduation from an NCAA Football Bowl Subdivision University," *International Journal of Sport Management* 11, no. 3 (2010): 477–91; Eric Olson, "Special Admissions Called 'Original Sin' of College Sports," *AP News*, March 16, 2019, https://apnews.com /article/a842ec11faa645b7adf5e75034e8bbf4.

16. Gerald S. Gurney, "Stop Lowering the Bar for College Athletes," *The Chronicle of Higher Education*, April 10, 2011, https://www.chronicle.com/article /stop-lowering-the-bar-for-college-athletes/.

17. Gerald S. Gurney and Jerome C. Weber, "A Better Way to Measure Coaches' Wins and Losses," *The Chronicle of Higher Education*, October 24, 2008, https:// www.chronicle.com/article/a-better-way-to-measure-coaches-wins-and-losses/.

18. Christian S. Dennie and Gerald S. Gurney, "It's Time for the NCAA to Get It Right," *The Chronicle of Higher Education*, January 8, 2012, https://www .chronicle.com/article/its-time-for-the-ncaa-to-get-it-right/.

19. Gerald S. Gurney, "Now We Must Reform Athletics Reform," *The Chronicle of Higher Education*, October 18, 2009, https://www.chronicle.com/article/now -we-must-reform-athletics-reform/.

20. Gerald S. Gurney and Jerome C. Weber, "Professors Must Speak Out: Colleges Can No Longer Afford Athletics as Usual," *The Chronicle of Higher Education*, April 5, 2010, https://www.chronicle.com/article/professors-must-speak -out-colleges-can-no-longer-afford-athletics-as-usual/.

21. Gerald S. Gurney, "Toughen NCAA Standards for Freshmen," *Inside Higher Ed*, February 6, 2011, https://www.insidehighered.com/views/2011/02/07/ toughen-ncaa-standards-freshmen.

22. NCAA, *Faculty Athletics Representative Handbook*, NCAA Faculty Athletics Representative Association (FARA), n.d., accessed February 15, 2024, https://www .ncaafara.org/_files/ugd/ad7e32_ed76dc0c17884b4c9f5f8fa41447993b.pdf.

A faculty athletic representative, or FAR, is required for each NCAA member institution. Duties of the FAR are determined by each school but can generally be characterized as serving as a liaison between the institution and the athletics department and also as a representative of the institution in conference and NCAA affairs. As stated in the FAR handbook, "Because student-athletes are to be students first, faculty voices and perspectives in the administration and oversight of intercollegiate athletic programs have been recognized with the NCAA as legitimate and necessary" (NCAA, *Faculty Athletics Representative Handbook*, 4). The main role of a FAR is to certify athletic eligibility. Only the FAR can be the final signature for any athlete's eligibility at an NCAA school. The FAR serves at the pleasure of the president or chancellor and is a liaison to the academic side of campus, often being the point person for eligibility and faculty/athlete disputes. Although this role does work well on many campuses, many FARs have had a reputation for being more interested in the athletic perks that come with the position, such as traveling to games, going to NCAA and conference functions, and receiving free athletic-related gear and gifts. Many have not stood up to the athletic machine and put academic integrity first. In other words, FARs generally have not prevented increased academic fraud and eligibility manipulation nor stood up for commonsense reform proposals (NCAA, *Faculty Athletics Representative Handbook*).

CHAPTER EIGHT

1. M. Chapman, B. Ridpath, and M. Denhart, "An Examination of Increased NCAA Division I Athletic Department Budgets: A Case Study of Student Perceptions of Fee Allocation for Athletes," *International Journal of Sport Management* 15, no. 1 (2014): 25–48; Steve Berkowitz, Jodi Upton, and Erik Brady, "Most NCAA Division I Athletic Departments Take Subsidies," *USA Today*, July 1, 2013, https://www.usatoday.com/story/sports/college/2013/05/07/ncaa-finances-subsidies/2142443/.

2. "Analysis: Who Is Winning in the High-Revenue World of College Sports?" *PBS NewsHour*. March 19, 2023. https://www.pbs.org/newshour/economy/analysis-who-is-winning-in-the-high-revenue-world-of-college-sports.

3. Taylor Branch, "The Shame of College Sports," *The Atlantic*, October 5, 2011, https://www.theatlantic.com/magazine/archive/2011/10/the-shame-of-college-sports/308643/.

4. Gerald S. Gurney and Jerome C. Weber, "A Better Way to Measure Coaches' Wins and Losses," *The Chronicle of Higher Education*, October 24, 2008, https://www.chronicle.com/article/a-better-way-to-measure-coaches-wins-and-losses/.

---

a. Matthew Denhart and Richard Vedder, "Intercollegiate Athletics Subsidies: A Regressive Tax," Center for College Affordability and Productivity, April 2010, https://files.eric.ed.gov/fulltext/ED536486.pdf; Chapman, Ridpath, and Denhart, "An Examination of Increased NCAA Division I Athletic Department Budgets"; Steve Berkowitz, Jodi Upton, and Erik Brady, "Most NCAA Division I Athletic Departments Take Subsidies," *USA Today*, July 1, 2013, https://www.usatoday.com/story/sports/college/2013/05/07/ncaa-finances-subsidies/2142443/.

b. Berkowitz, Upton, and Brady, "Most NCAA Division I Athletic Departments Take Subsidies"; "How Student Fees Boost College Sports amid Rising Budgets," Knight Commission on Intercollegiate Athletics, September 23, 2010, https://www.knightcommission.org/2010/09/how-student-fees-boost-college-sports-amid-rising-budgets/.

CHAPTER NINE

1. Gerald Gurney, Donna Lopiano, and Andrew Zimbalist, "Academic Integrity," chapter 3 in *Unwinding Madness: What Went Wrong with College Sports and How to Fix It* (Washington, DC: Brookings Institute, 2017).

2. Gerald S. Gurney, "Stop Lowering the Bar for College Athletes," *The Chronicle of Higher Education*, April 10, 2011, https://www.chronicle.com/article/stop-lowering-the-bar-for-college-athletes/; Gerald S. Gurney, David Tan, and Carla Winters, "Specially Admitted Student-Athletes: Their Academic Performance, Persistence, and Graduation from an NCAA Football Bowl Subdivision University," *International Journal of Sport Management* 11, no. 3 (2010): 477–91; Eric Olson, "Special Admissions Called 'Original Sin' of College Sports," *AP News*, March 16, 2019, https://apnews.com/article/a842ec11faa645b7adf5e75034e8bbf4.

3. Gurney, Lopiano, and Zimbalist, "Academic Integrity"; Carla A. Winters and Gerald S. Gurney, "Academic Preparation of Specially-Admitted Student-Athletes: A Question of Basic Skills," *College and University* 88, no. 2 (2012): 2–9; Brad Wolverton, "Spending Plenty So Athletes Can Make the Grade," *The Chronicle of Higher Education*, September 5, 2008, https://www.chronicle.com/article/spending-plenty-so-athletes-can-make-the-grade/.

4. Jeffrey Fountain and Peter Finley, "Academic Clustering: A Longitudinal Analysis of a Division I Football Program," *Journal of Issues in Intercollegiate Athletics* 4 (2011) 24–41, https://scholarcommons.sc.edu/cgi/viewcontent.cgi?article=1050&context=jiia; Matthew R. Salzwedel and Jon Ericson, "Cleaning Up Buckley: How the Family Educational Rights and Privacy Act Shields Academic Corruption in College Athletics," *Wisconsin Law Review* (2003): 1053, https://heinonline.org/HOL/LandingPage?handle=hein.journals/wlr2003&div=41&id=&page=.

5. John Heuser, Dave Gershman, and Jim Carty, "University of Michigan Athletes'Safe Harbor'Is General Studies," *Ann Arbor News*, March 18, 2008, https://www.mlive.com/wolverines/academics/stories/2008/03/athletes_safe_harbor_is_genera.html; Jay M. Smith and Mary Willingham, *Cheated: The UNC Scandal, the Education of Athletes, and the Future of Big-Time College Sports* (University of Nebraska Press, 2019); Pete Thamel, "Top Grades and No Class Time for Auburn Players," *New York Times*, July 14, 2006, https://www.nytimes.com/2006/07/14/sports/ncaafootball/14auburn.html.

Several scandals erupted as colleges and universities built new academic centers and created path-of-least-resistance academic pathways to keep athletes eligible. Some of these pathways involved academic majors usually labeled as general or interdisciplinary studies or majors with more academic-sounding names that were primarily filled by athletes. Other scandals included credit for classes that required little to no work or that were essentially independent studies. Notable examples of such scandals include those at Auburn University, the University of Michigan, and the University of North Carolina.

---

a. Gerald Gurney, Lisa Rubin, Sarah Stokowski, and B. David Ridpath, "The Original Sin of College Sports: College Presidents' Ineffectual Use of Special Admissions," *Journal of NCAA Compliance*, May–June 2020, https://tigerprints .clemson.edu/cgi/viewcontent.cgi?article=1017&context=ed_org_ldrshp_pub.

b. Brad Wolverton, "Spending Plenty So Athletes Can Make the Grade," *The Chronicle of Higher Education*, September 5, 2008, https://www.chronicle.com /article/spending-plenty-so-athletes-can-make-the-grade/.

CHAPTER TEN

1. "About N4A," National Association of Collegiate Directors of Athletics (N4A), accessed February 15, 2024, https://nacda.com/sports/2018/7/17/nfoura -aboutus-html.aspx.

2. The NCAA Division I Academic Cabinet oversees all academic matters not addressed by the NCAA Committee on Academic Performance. The Academic Cabinet reports to the Division I Leadership Council on policy issues. NCAA committees that report to the Academic Cabinet include the International Student Records Committee, High School Review Committee, Student Records Review Committee, Initial-Eligibility Waiver Committee, Progress-toward-Degree Committee, and Progress-toward-Degree Waiver Committee ("Division I Academic Cabinet").

3. The Coalition on Intercollegiate Athletics (COIA) is an alliance of faculty senates from NCAA Division I schools. COIA's mission is to provide a national faculty voice on intercollegiate sports issues. Areas of concern include academic integrity and quality, student-athlete welfare, campus governance of intercollegiate athletics, commercialization, and fiscal responsibility. The coalition is committed to the development of effective strategies and proposals for significant, long-term reform in college athletics. COIA works with university faculties, administrations, and national associations concerned with higher education to implement these strategies and proposals. The main difference between COIA and other faculty-led groups like The Drake Group is that COIA is committed to working through the NCAA-established processes to enact reform rather than facilitating change from the outside through the courts, legislation, or athletes' rights ("COIA: Coalition on Intercollegiate Athletics").

4. Eric Olson, "Special Admissions Called 'Original Sin' of College Sports," *AP News*, March 16, 2019, https://apnews.com/article/a842ec11faa645b7adf 5e75034e8bbf4.

5. Dr. Jon Ericson, the former provost at Drake University, founded The Drake Group (TDG) on October 23, 1999, as a faculty-driven group with the goal of improving academic integrity in college sports. TDG emerged from a two-day

meeting in Des Moines, Iowa, where Ericson invited a distinguished group of college faculty, authors, and activists to a twenty-four-hour session to discuss how to end academic corruption in college sports. Included in the conference were members of faculty senates, journalists, athletic directors, and members of organizations such as the NCAA and the Knight Commission on Intercollegiate Athletics. This meeting resulted in a reform proposal to enact a program of academic disclosure at all NCAA schools—publicly disclosing, in aggregate, the majors and enrolled courses (and associated faculty) of athletes in comparison to the rest of the student body (Salzwedel and Ericson, "Cleaning Up Buckley"). As TDG founder and first president, Ericson led an aggressive campaign for disclosure as the only realistic way to restore academic integrity in collegiate sports—arguing that teaching and grading practices should be open to public scrutiny and sharing this information in aggregate is not a violation of the Family Education Rights and Privacy Act (FERPA) (also known as the Buckley Amendment). In September 2022, TDG established a sister organization, The Drake Group Education Fund under the fiscal 501(c)(3) sponsorship of the Players Philanthropy Fund (PPF). PPF will host The Drake Group Education Fund until the new organization's application for its own 501(c)(3) status is approved. Taking this action better positions TDG to focus on its priority mission of influencing Congress and other legislative policymakers to address the serious academic, health, and economic crises in intercollegiate athletics ("History—The Drake Group, Inc.").

6. The College Sports Research Institute (CSRI) was the brainchild of Dr. Richard Southall and several Drake Group members in the early 2000s. Yet, it was the NCAA that essentially forced the creation of CSRI as an independent college sports research organization by canceling its sponsorship for such research ("About CSRI—College Sport Research Institute"). In 2007, the NCAA planned an NCAA Research Colloquium and sponsored an academic journal, *The Journal of Intercollegiate Sport*. Many members of The Drake Group, including Southall as an abstract reviewer, were solicited to help with the colloquium. However, then-NCAA President Myles Brand abruptly canceled the colloquium ostensibly because the submitted research was largely critical of the NCAA and its academic reform efforts. Nevertheless, the colloquium returned in 2008 and continued until 2012 before the NCAA discontinued it, claiming it did not meet its stated goals. Many believed the discontinuation was due to the nature of the research, which was continually critical of the NCAA and its operations. This series of events led Southall to establish CSRI at the University of Memphis, where he hosted the first academic conference in 2008 and launched a new academic journal, *Journal of Issues in Intercollegiate Athletics*. CSRI later moved to the University of North Carolina and then the University of South Carolina (Steinbach, "Scholars React to Cancellation of NCAA Colloquium").

CHAPTER ELEVEN

1. Gerald Gurney, Donna Lopiano, and Andrew Zimbalist, "How College Sports Lost Its Way I" and "How College Sports Lost Its Way II," chaps. 1 and 2 in *Unwinding Madness: What Went Wrong with College Sports and How to Fix It* (Washington, DC: Brookings Institute, 2017); Taylor Branch, "The Shame of College Sports," *The Atlantic*, October 5, 2011, https://www.theatlantic.com /magazine/archive/2011/10/the-shame-of-college-sports/308643/.

2. Presidents and chancellors of colleges and universities are the entities in charge of the intercollegiate athletic enterprise as codified in NCAA rules. Article 6, Institutional Control, denotes that control and responsibility for the conduct of intercollegiate athletics shall be exercised by the institution itself and the division and conference of which it is a member. A member institution's president or chancellor has ultimate responsibility and final authority for the conduct of the intercollegiate athletics program and the actions of any board in control of that program (*NCAA 2023–24 Division I Manual*).

3. The Knight Commission on Intercollegiate Athletics is an independent group with a legacy of leading reforms that strengthen the educational mission of college sports. Established by the John S. and James L. Knight Foundation in October 1989, the commission created a reform agenda in response to highly visible athletics scandals and low graduation rates among college football and men's basketball players, which threatened the integrity of higher education. The commission includes current and former university presidents and chancellors, university trustees, former college athletes, and nationally recognized thought leaders from organizations connected to higher education or college sports. According to the Knight Commission website, its purpose is to develop, promote, and lead transformational change that prioritizes the education, health, safety, and success of college athletes ("About the Knight Commission").

4. Gurney, Lopiano, and Zimbalist, "The NCAA's Unsustainable Economics," chap. 7 in *Unwinding Madness*; Michael H. Leroy, "College Athletic Debt Soars as Power 5 Programs Resist Scrutiny," *Sportico*, January 5, 2022, https://www.sportico .com/leagues/college-sports/2022/college-athletic-debt-soars-1234651231/.

5. Though $9 million was the average debt for Division I athletic departments when this manuscript was written, debt service has only increased as NCAA Division I universities continue to spend unabated—mostly due to new facility construction and renovation. According to Sportico's 2019–2020 NCAA institutional financial reports, the University of Iowa led the nation in paying "facilities debt service" ($32,599,749) followed by The Ohio State University ($29,748,769), University of Alabama ($23,822,661), Texas A&M University ($23,454,394), Michigan State University ($21,484,385), University of Texas ($20,765,071), University of Illinois ($19,007,456), University of Oregon ($18,720,155), and University of Michigan ($17,358,525) (Leroy, "College Athletic Debt Soars").

6. Steve Berkowitz, Jodi Upton, and Christopher Schnaars, "It's Academic: Coaches, ADs Collect APR Bonuses," *USA Today*, June 11, 2013, https://www .usatoday.com/story/sports/college/2013/06/11/ncaa-apr-bonuses-coach-athletics -director/2412095/; D. B. Ridpath, B. Porto, G. Gurney, D. Lopiano, A. Sack, M. Willingham, and A. Zimbalist, "The Drake Group Position Statement: Student Fee Allocations to Fund Intercollegiate Athletics," March 2, 2015, https://www .thedrakegroupeducationfund.org/wp-content/uploads/2019/06/position-state ment-student-fees-final-3-2-15.pdf; Matthew Denhart and Richard Vedder, "Intercollegiate Athletics Subsidies: A Regressive Tax," Center for College Affordability and Productivity, April 2010, https://files.eric.ed.gov/fulltext/ ED536486.pdf.

Many believe that all Division I college athletics departments make a profit and generate their own revenues. This is only true for ten to twenty of the top Division I schools. The rest are largely paid for through student fees and other institutional subsidies (Ridpath, Porto, Gurney, Lopiano, Sack, Willingham, and Zimbalist, "The Drake Group Position Statement").

7. "Restoring the Balance: Dollars, Values, and the Future of College Sports," Knight Commission on Intercollegiate Athletics, 2017, https://www.knightcom mission.org/wp-content/uploads/2017/09/restoring-the-balance-0610-01.pdf.

8. The Knight Commission survey of Division I presidents and chancellors found the majority of NCAA Division I campus and sports leaders believe that college sports reform should be focused on "big solutions," and revealed wide dis-satisfaction with current Division I governance along with their admitted inability to control it even though they are ultimately responsible ("Groundbreaking Knight Commission Survey Finds Division I Leaders Overwhelmingly Support Major Reform").

9. An investigation by *NorthJersey.com* revealed that, since joining the Big Ten in 2014, Rutgers University funneled nearly half a billion dollars into ath-letics from loans, tuition revenue, student fees, and taxpayer dollars. Top Rutgers administrators hid this fact. Against NCAA guidelines, management reported certain loans to the athletics program as revenue, violating university policy by doling out more than $80 million in university loans to finance athletic pro-gram operating deficits. James M. O'Neill, "Rutgers Athletics Spends Big— and Builds Big Debt—to Stay Competitive in the Big Ten." *NorthJersey.com*, July 7, 2022, https://www.northjersey.com/story/news/watchdog/2022/07/07/ rutgers-athletics-spends-big-builds-debt-big-ten-conference/65367819007/.

10. M. Chapman, B. Ridpath, and M. Denhart, "An Examination of Increased NCAA Division I Athletic Department Budgets: A Case Study of Student Perceptions of Fee Allocation for Athletes," *International Journal of Sport Management* 15, no. 1 (2014): 25–48.

11. Jake New, "What CEOs Don't Know. Big-Time Colleges Were Rushing to Hire Executives as Athletics Directors a Few Years Ago—

but the Results Have Some Questioning the Trend," *Inside Higher Ed*, November 6, 2014, https://www.insidehighered.com/news/2014/11/07/colleges -turn-athletics-directors-business-background-results-vary#.

12. Brian Bennett, "College Football—Facilities Arms Race Proves Recession-Proof," *ESPN.com*, June 14, 2012, https://www.espn.com/college-football/story/_/ id/8047787/college-football-facilities-arms-race-proves-recession-proof.

CHAPTER TWELVE

1. Gerald Gurney, Donna Lopiano, and Andrew Zimbalist, "How College Sports Lost Its Way I," chap. 1 in *Unwinding Madness: What Went Wrong with College Sports and How to Fix It* (Washington, DC: Brookings Institute, 2017); Andrew Zimbalist, "Sports Hiatus Gives NCAA an Opportunity to Rethink the Structure of College Sports," *Forbes*, April 25, 2020, https://www.forbes.com/sites /andrewzimbalist/2020/04/25/sports-being-on-hiatus-gives-ncaa-an-opportunity -to-rethink-the-structure-of-college-sports/?sh=2dd34e4c3b54.

2. The Tax Cuts and Jobs Act, a US tax reform bill, signed into law in 2018, repealed a rule that allowed taxpayers to deduct 80 percent of a contribution made for the right to purchase tickets to college and university athletic events. However, there are still many ways for donors to receive tax breaks for donating to college athletic programs under the guise and tax protections of education donations (Flahaven, "The College Athletic Seating Deduction Is Out").

3. "Drake Group Calls for Congress to Enact College Athlete Protections: A Legislative Proposal," The Drake Group Education Fund, September 8, 2020, https://www.thedrakegroup.org/2020/09/08/drake-group-calls-for-congress-to -enact-college-athlete-protections-a-legislative-proposal/.

---

a. "Examine Current Sports Bills before Congress." The Drake Group Education Fund, updated October 16, 2023, https://www.thedrakegroupeducation fund.org/2022/04/12/examine-current-sport-bills-before-congress/.

b. "The Drake Group Strongly Supports 'College Athletes Bill of Rights' Introduced in the 117th Congress," The Drake Group Education Fund, August 18, 2022, https://www.thedrakegroupeducationfund.org/2020/12/21/the-drake -group-strongly-supports-college-athletes-bill-of-rights-introduced-in-the -117th-congress/.

CHAPTER THIRTEEN

1. Jay M. Smith and Mary Willingham, *Cheated: The UNC Scandal, the Education of Athletes, and the Future of Big-Time College Sports* (University of Nebraska Press, 2019).

2. "A Real Incentive or PR?" *Inside Higher Ed*, 2015, https://www.insidehigh ered.com/news/2015/02/06/academic-requirements-coaching-bonuses-rare; Steve Berkowitz, Jodi Upton, and Christopher Schnaars, "It's Academic: Coaches, ADs Collect APR Bonuses." *USA Today*, June 11, 2013, https://www.usatoday.com/story /sports/college/2013/06/11/ncaa-apr-bonuses-coach-athletics-director/2412095/.

For years, NCAA coaches have received incentive payments in addition to their salaries, typically in the form of bonuses for achieving competitive milestones such as winning games, participating in bowl games, or making the postseason. Recently, and controversially, these bonuses have increasingly been tied to academic benchmarks like Academic Progress Rate (APR) scores, minimum grade point averages, and graduation rates. All are noted throughout this book as highly suspect and/or invalid measurements of academic primacy. Many scholars and others argue that these incentive payments serve more as public relations tools, creating an illusion that academics are as valued as winning in college sports. While some of these bonuses extend to athletic staff members, typically athletic directors, they rarely reach academic support staff. The practice of awarding bonuses for athlete academic performance became more prevalent following the introduction of the APR (2008–2009). High-profile supporters, such as former US Secretary of Education Arne Duncan, advocated for more stringent measures. In 2011, Duncan proposed that teams failing to meet the minimum APR should be banned from tournaments or bowl games, thereby eliminating the possibility of coaching bonuses for championship appearances. Later that year, the NCAA Division I Board of Directors adopted this approach. In 2013, Duncan, along with former Congressman and basketball player Tom McMillen, co-wrote an opinion piece for *USA Today* urging colleges to "financially punish coaches" who do not graduate at least half of their athletes. They argued, "Poor academic performance means the team or the individual player—not the coach—gets punished. But no coach should receive financial bonuses when much of his team is flunking out or failing to get a degree" (Duncan and McMillen, "Want to Change College Athletics?").

3. Eric Kelderman, "Who Should Oversee Athletes' Academic Progress?" *The Chronicle of Higher Education*, January 28, 2018, https://www.chronicle.com/ article/who-should-oversee-athletes-academic-progress/; B. David Ridpath, Gerald S. Gurney, and Eric M. Snyder, "NCAA Academic Fraud Cases and Historical Consistency: A Comparative Content Analysis." *Journal of the Legal Aspects of Sport* 25, no. 2 (2015): 75–103, https://doi.org/10.1123/jlas.2014-0021.

4. Gerald Gurney, Donna Lopiano, and Andrew Zimbalist, "Academic Integrity," chap. 3 in *Unwinding Madness: What Went Wrong with College Sports and How to Fix It* (Washington, DC: Brookings Institute, 2017); G. Gurney, E. Lopiano, D. Snyder, M. Willingham, J. Meyer, B. Porto, D. B. Ridpath, A. Sack, and A. Zimbalist, "The Drake Group Education Fund Position Statement: Why the NCAA Academic Progress Rate (APR) and Graduation Success Rate (GSR) Should Be Abandoned and Replaced with More Effective

Academic Metrics." 2015. https://thedrakegroupeducationfund.org/2015/06/07/drake-group-questions-ncaa-academic-metrics/.

5. Gurney, Lopiano, and Zimbalist, "How College Sports Lost Its Way I," chap. 1 in *Unwinding Madness*; Gerald S. Gurney and Jerome C. Weber, "Professors Must Speak Out: Colleges Can No Longer Afford Athletics as Usual," *The Chronicle of Higher Education*, April 5, 2010, https://www.chronicle.com/article/professors-must-speak-out-colleges-can-no-longer-afford-athletics-as-usual/.

6. Mark Memmott, "Report: Years and Years of Missed Chances in Penn State Scandal," *NPR*, November 14, 2011, https://www.npr.org/sections/thetwo-way/2011/11/14/142298661/report-years-and-years-of-missed-chances-in-penn-state-scandal.

7. Dennis Dodd, "The Pac-12 Is Dead as We Know It, Just Don't Expect the Big Ten, Big 12 or Anyone Else to Take the Blame," CBS Sports, August 4, 2023, https://www.cbssports.com/college-football/news/the-pac-12-is-dead-as-we-know-it-just-dont-expect-the-big-ten-big-12-or-anyone-else-to-take-the-blame/.

The super-conference phenomenon is currently underway, with the Big Ten and Southeastern Conference (SEC) expanding by adding top college football teams. The SEC has welcomed Oklahoma and Texas, while the Big Ten has added UCLA, USC, Washington, and Oregon. Aiming to remain competitive as super-conferences, the Atlantic Coast Conference (ACC) and the Big 12 Conference have also recruited teams seeking better financial returns. Meanwhile, the Pacific 12 (PAC 12)—a college athletic conference for more than one hundred years, known as the Conference of Champions—struggled with lower television and streaming revenue compared to other conferences. This financial shortfall led to teams moving to other conferences (Dodd, "The Pac-12 Is Dead as We Know It").

---

a. "Awards," The Drake Group Education Fund, 2016, https://www.thedrakegroupeducationfund.org/events-awards/awards/.

b. Phil Rosenthal, "So Much for Chicago's Big Ten Team: 75 Years Ago, the University of Chicago Told the Conference It Wanted Out," *Chicago Tribune*, March 9, 2021, https://www.chicagotribune.com/2021/03/08/so-much-for-chicagos-big-ten-team-75-years-ago-the-university-of-chicago-told-the-conference-it-wanted-out/.

c. Eric Kelderman, "Who Should Oversee Athletes' Academic Progress?" *The Chronicle of Higher Education*, January 28, 2018, https://www.chronicle.com/article/who-should-oversee-athletes-academic-progress/.

CHAPTER FOURTEEN

1. In August 2003, the Division I Board of Directors and NCAA Executive Committee established the Student-Athlete Opportunity Fund with a pool of $17

million ("Financial Aid—Student-Athlete Opportunity Fund"; "Student-Athlete Opportunity Fund (SAOF)"). This fund is allocated to athletic conferences based on sports sponsorship and grants-in-aid and is intended to assist athletes with various expenses related to athletics or academic achievement. The primary purpose of the fund is to offer flexibility to athletes in covering costs associated with their participation in sports and to support their academic success. The fund aims to provide additional benefits directly to athletes or their families, as determined by individual conference offices and the NCAA. All college athletes, including international students, are eligible for these benefits, regardless of scholarship status, demonstrated need, or whether they have exhausted their eligibility or no longer participate due to medical reasons.

EPILOGUE

1. Ross Finkel, Trevor Martin, and Jon Paley, directors, *Schooled: The Price of College Sports* (Makuhari Media, 2013).

2. Gerald Gurney, interview, *Real Sports with Bryant Gumbel*, season 20, episode 3, "Gaming the System," HBO, March 25, 2014.

3. Gerald Gurney, interview, *The Bob Edwards Show*, "Dropping the Ball: The Shady Side of Big-Time College Sports," SiriusXM Satellite Radio, September 22, 2014.

4. Gerald Gurney, Ramogi Huma, Ellen Staurowsky, and Mary Willingham, "How Colleges Cheat Student-Athletes," Senate panel hosted by Senator Chris Murphy, Washington, DC, July 25, 2019, https://www.facebook.com /senchrismurphy/videos/480132192387869?s=1027693677&v=e&sfns=mo.

5. Gerald Gurney, Donna Lopiano, and Andrew Zimbalist, preface to *Unwinding Madness: What Went Wrong with College Sports and How to Fix It* (Washington, DC: Brookings Institute, 2017).

6. Jay M. Smith and Mary Willingham, *Cheated: The UNC Scandal, the Education of Athletes, and the Future of Big-Time College Sports* (University of Nebraska Press, 2019).

7. Gurney, Lopiano, and Zimbalist, *Unwinding Madness*.

BIBLIOGRAPHY

Bibliography and notes compiled by Dr. B. David Ridpath, EdD.

"About CSRI—College Sport Research Institute." College Sport Research Institute. Accessed February 15, 2024. https://www.csri.org/about-us.

"About FARs." NCAA. Accessed February 15, 2024. https://www.ncaafara.org/copy-of-fara-leadership.

"About N4A." National Association of Collegiate Directors of Athletics (N4A). Accessed February 15, 2024. https://nacda.com/sports/2018/7/17/nfoura-aboutus-html.aspx.

"About the Knight Commission." Knight Commission on Intercollegiate Athletics. May 9, 2022. https://www.knightcommission.org/about-knight-commission/.

"Analysis: Who Is Winning in the High-Revenue World of College Sports?" *PBS NewsHour*, March 19, 2023. https://www.pbs.org/newshour/economy/analysis-who-is-winning-in-the-high-revenue-world-of-college-sports.

"Awards." The Drake Group Education Fund. 2016. https://www.thedrakegroupeducationfund.org/events-awards/awards/.

Bennett, Brian. "College Football—Facilities Arms Race Proves Recession-Proof." *ESPN.com*, June 14, 2012. https://www.espn.com/college-football/story/_/id/8047787/college-football-facilities-arms-race-proves-recession-proof.

Berkowitz, Steve, Jodi Upton, and Erik Brady. "Most NCAA Division I Athletic Departments Take Subsidies." *USA Today*, July 1, 2013. https://www.usatoday.com/story/sports/college/2013/05/07/ncaa-finances-subsidies/2142443/.

Berkowitz, Steve, Jodi Upton, and Christopher Schnaars. "It's Academic: Coaches, ADs Collect APR Bonuses." *USA Today*, June 11, 2013. https://www.usatoday.com/story/sports/college/2013/06/11/ncaa-apr-bonuses-coach-athletics-director/2412095/.

Branch, Taylor. "The Shame of College Sports." *The Atlantic*, October 5, 2011. https://www.theatlantic.com/magazine/archive/2011/10/the-shame-of-college-sports/308643/.

Byers, Walter. *Unsportsmanlike Conduct: Exploiting College Athletes*. University of Michigan Press, 1995.

"Bylaw, Article 19 Infractions Program." NCAA. Accessed February 15, 2024. https://web3.ncaa.org/lsdbi/search/bylawView?id=11781.

"Bylaws, Article 17 Playing and Practice Seasons." NCAA. Accessed February 15, 2024. https://web3.ncaa.org/lsdbi/search/bylawView?id=8823.

Chapman, M., B. Ridpath, and M. Denhart. "An Examination of Increased NCAA Division I Athletic Department Budgets: A Case Study of Student Perceptions of Fee Allocation for Athletes." *International Journal of Sport Management* 15, no. 1 (2014): 25–48.

Christianson, Eric, and Hollie Geren. "NCAA Launches Latest Public Service Announcements, Introduces New Student-Focused Website." NCAA news release, March 13, 2007. http://fs.ncaa.org/Docs/PressArchive/2007/Announcements/NCAA%2BLaunches%2BLatest%2BPublic%2BService%2BAnnouncements%2BIntroduces%2BNew%2BStudent-Focused%2BWebsite.html.

"COIA: Coalition on Intercollegiate Athletics." Coalition on Intercollegiate Athletics. Accessed February 15, 2024. https://www.thecoia.org/.

Cureton v. National Collegiate Athletic Association, 37 F. Supp. 2d 687 (E.D. Pa. 1999).

Denhart, Matthew, and Richard Vedder. "Intercollegiate Athletics Subsidies: A Regressive Tax." Center for College Affordability and Productivity, April 2010. https://files.eric.ed.gov/fulltext/ED536486.pdf.

Dennie, Christian S., and Gerald S. Gurney. "It's Time for the NCAA to Get It Right." *The Chronicle of Higher Education*, January 8, 2012. https://www.chronicle.com/article/its-time-for-the-ncaa-to-get-it-right/.

"Division I Academic Cabinet." NCAA.org. November 16, 2013. https://www.ncaa.org/sports/2013/11/16/division-i-academic-cabinet.aspx.

"Division I Academic Progress Rate (APR)." NCAA, November 20, 2013. https://www.ncaa.org/sports/2013/11/20/division-i-academic-progress-rate-apr.aspx.

Dodd, Dennis. "The Pac-12 Is Dead as We Know It, Just Don't Expect the Big Ten, Big 12 or Anyone Else to Take the Blame." CBS Sports, August 4, 2023. https://www.cbssports.com/college-football/news/the-pac-12-is-dead-as-we-know-it-just-dont-expect-the-big-ten-big-12-or-anyone-else-to-take-the-blame/.

Dodd, Dennis. "30 Years Later: The Legacy of SMU's Death Penalty and Six Teams Nearly Hit with One," CBS Sports, February 22, 2017. https://www

.cbssports.com/college-football/news/30-years-later-the-legacy-of-smus
-death-penalty-and-six-teams-nearly-hit-with-one/.

"Drake Group Calls for Congress to Enact College Athlete Protections: A Legislative Proposal." The Drake Group Education Fund. September 8, 2020. https://www.thedrakegroup.org/2020/09/08/drake-group-calls-for-congress
-to-enact-college-athlete-protections-a-legislative-proposal/.

"The Drake Group Strongly Supports 'College Athletes Bill of Rights' Introduced in the 117th Congress." The Drake Group Education Fund. August 18, 2022. https://www.thedrakegroupeducationfund.org/2020/12/21/the-drake
-group-strongly-supports-college-athletes-bill-of-rights-introduced-in-the
-117th-congress/.

Duncan, Arne, and Tom McMillen. "Want to Change College Athletics? Financially Punish Coaches." *USA Today*, March 22, 2013. https://www
.usatoday.com/story/sports/ncaab/2013/03/20/arne-duncan-tom-mcmillen
-march-madness-education-coach-salaries/2004835/.

"Enforcement: Division I Internal Operating Procedures." NCAA. 2023. https://
ncaaorg.s3.amazonaws.com/enforcement/d1/D1ENF_EnforcementIOPs
.pdf.

"Examine Current Sports Bills before Congress." The Drake Group Education Fund. Updated October 16, 2023. https://www.thedrakegroupeducationfund
.org/2022/04/12/examine-current-sport-bills-before-congress/.

Falla, Jack. NCAA: The Voice of College Sports. Mission, KN: National Collegiate Athletic Association, 1981.

"Financial Aid—Student-Athlete Opportunity Fund." NCAA. Accessed February 15, 2024. https://web3.ncaa.org/lsdbi/search/proposalView?id=863.

Finkel, Ross, Trevor Martin, and Jon Paley, directors. *Schooled: The Price of College Sports*. Makuhari Media, 2013.

Flahaven, Brian. "The College Athletic Seating Deduction Is Out. Here's What We Know (So Far)." CASE Blog, January 26, 2018. https://blog
.case.org/2018/01/26/the-college-athletic-seating-deduction-is-out
-heres-what-we-know-so-far/.

Florek, Michael. "A Breakdown of All the Big Bonuses Big 12, SEC Football Coaches Received This Season." *Dallas Morning News*, January 23, 2016. https://www.dallasnews.com/sports/2016/01/23/a-breakdown-of-all-the
-big-bonuses-big-12-sec-football-coaches-received-this-season/.

"For Faculty Who Have Student-Athletes in Class." University of North Carolina at Chapel Hill. Accessed February 15, 2024. https://aspsa.unc.edu
/for-faculty-who-have-student-athletes-in-class.

Fountain, Jeffrey, and Peter Finley. "Academic Clustering: A Longitudinal Analysis of a Division I Football Program." *Journal of Issues in Intercollegiate Athletics* 4 (2011): 24–41. https://scholarcommons.sc.edu/cgi/viewcontent.cgi?article=1050&context=jiia.

Frank, Robert. "New Study Debunks Link among Winning College Athletic Programs and Increases in Donations and Quality of Applicants." Knight Commission on Intercollegiate Athletics. September 7, 2004. https://www.knightcommission.org/2004/09/new-study-debunks-link-among-winning-college-athletic-programs-and-increases-in-donations-and-quality-of-applicants/.

Gaston-Gayles, Joy L. "Advising Student Athletes: An Examination of Academic Support Programs with High Graduation Rates," *NACADA Journal* 23, nos. 1–2 (2003): 50–57.

Gaul, Gilbert M. *Billion-Dollar Ball: A Journey through the Big-Money Culture of College Football*. Penguin, 2015.

Gerdy, John R. *The Successful College Athletic Program: The New Standard*. Oryx Press, 1997.

Goldstein, Amy. "Wade Quits after Rocky Three-Year Stint as Coach." *Washington Post*, May 13, 1989. https://www.washingtonpost.com/wp-srv/sports/longterm/memories/bias/launch/wadeq.htm.

"Graduation Rates." NCAA. 2013. https://www.ncaa.org/sports/2013/11/19/graduation-rates.aspx.

"Groundbreaking Knight Commission Survey Finds Division I Leaders Overwhelmingly Support Major Reform." Knight Commission on Intercollegiate Athletics. September 26, 2022. https://www.knightcommission.org/2020/10/groundbreaking-knight-commission-survey-finds-division-i-leaders-overwhelmingly-support-major-reform/.

Gurney, G., E. Lopiano, D. Snyder, M. Willingham, J. Meyer, B. Porto, D. B. Ridpath, A. Sack, and A. Zimbalist. "The Drake Group Education Fund Position Statement: Why the NCAA Academic Progress Rate (APR) and Graduation Success Rate (GSR) Should Be Abandoned and Replaced with More Effective Academic Metrics." The Drake Group Education Fund. 2015. https://thedrakegroupeducationfund.org/2015/06/07/drake-group-questions-ncaa-academic-metrics/.

Gurney, Gerald. Interview. *The Bob Edwards Show*. "Dropping the Ball: The Shady Side of Big-Time College Sports." SiriusXM Satellite Radio, September 22, 2014.

Gurney, Gerald. Interview. *Real Sports with Bryant Gumbel*. Season 20, episode 3, "Gaming the System." HBO, March 25, 2014.

Gurney, Gerald, Woodrow Eckard, and Richard Southall. "The Hoax of NCAA Graduation Rates." *Sports Litigation Alert*, December 22, 2017. https://sports litigationalert.com/the-hoax-of-ncaa-graduation-rates/.

Gurney, Gerald, Ramogi Huma, Ellen Staurowsky, and Mary Willingham. "How Colleges Cheat Student-Athletes." Senate panel hosted by Senator Chris Murphy. Washington, DC, July 25, 2019. https://www.facebook.com /senchrismurphy/videos/480132192387869?s=1027693677&v=e&sfns=mo.

Gurney, Gerald, Donna Lopiano, and Andrew Zimbalist. *Unwinding Madness: What Went Wrong with College Sports and How to Fix It*. Washington, DC: Brookings Institute, 2017.

Gurney, Gerald, Lisa Rubin, Sarah Stokowski, and B. David Ridpath. "The Original Sin of College Sports: College Presidents' Ineffectual Use of Special Admissions." *Journal of NCAA Compliance*, May–June 2020. https://tigerprints .clemson.edu/cgi/viewcontent.cgi?article=1017&context=ed_org_ldrshp_pub.

Gurney, Gerald, and Richard M. Southall. "NCAA Reform Gone Wrong." *Inside Higher Ed*, February 13, 2013, https://www.insidehighered.com /views/2013/02/14/ncaa-academic-reform-has-hurt-higher-eds-integrity -essay.

Gurney, Gerald, and Mary Willingham. "Academic Fraud, Athletes and Faculty Responsibility." *Inside Higher Ed*, July 17, 2014. https://www .insidehighered.com/views/2014/07/18/professors-must-take-academic -fraud-among-athletes-more-seriously-essay.

Gurney, Gerald S. "Now We Must Reform Athletics Reform." *The Chronicle of Higher Education*, October 18, 2009. https://www.chronicle.com/article /now-we-must-reform-athletics-reform/.

Gurney, Gerald S. "Stop Lowering the Bar for College Athletes." *The Chronicle of Higher Education*, April 10, 2011. https://www.chronicle.com/article /stop-lowering-the-bar-for-college-athletes/.

Gurney, Gerald S. "Toughen NCAA Standards for Freshmen." *Inside Higher Ed*, February 6, 2011. https://www.insidehighered.com/views/2011/02/07 /toughen-ncaa-standards-freshmen.

Gurney, Gerald S., and Richard M. Southall. "College Sports' Bait and Switch." *ESPN*, August 9, 2012. https://www.espn.com/college-sports/story/_/id /8248046/college-sports-programs-find-multitude-ways-game-ncaa-apr.

Gurney, Gerald S., David Tan, and Carla Winters. "Specially Admitted Student-Athletes: Their Academic Performance, Persistence, and Graduation from an NCAA Football Bowl Subdivision University." *International Journal of Sport Management* 11, no. 3 (2010): 477–91.

Gurney, Gerald S., and Jerome C. Weber. "A Better Way to Measure Coaches' Wins and Losses." *The Chronicle of Higher Education*, October 24, 2008. https://www.chronicle.com/article/a-better-way-to-measure-coaches-wins-and-losses/.

Gurney, Gerald S., and Jerome C. Weber. "Professors Must Speak Out: Colleges Can No Longer Afford Athletics as Usual." *The Chronicle of Higher Education*, April 5, 2010. https://www.chronicle.com/article/professors-must-speak-out-colleges-can-no-longer-afford-athletics-as-usual/.

Heuser, John, Dave Gershman, and Jim Carty. "University of Michigan Athletes' 'Safe Harbor' Is General Studies." *Ann Arbor News*, March 18, 2008. https://www.mlive.com/wolverines/academics/stories/2008/03/athletes_safe_harbor_is_genera.html.

"History—The Drake Group, Inc." The Drake Group. August 22, 2023. https://www.thedrakegroup.org/about/history/.

Hoover, John E. 2022. "Oklahoma in the Early Phases of Building a New $175 Million Football Facility." *Sports Illustrated Oklahoma Sooners News*, September 1, 2022. https://www.si.com/college/oklahoma/football/oklahoma-in-the-early-phases-of-building-a-new-175-million-football-facility.

"How Student Fees Boost College Sports amid Rising Budgets." Knight Commission on Intercollegiate Athletics. September 23, 2010. https://www.knightcommission.org/2010/09/how-student-fees-boost-college-sports-amid-rising-budgets/.

Huml, Matt R., N. David Pifer, Caitlin Towle, and Cheryl Rode. "Do Facilities Really Matter in Recruiting?" Athletic Director U. 2018. https://athleticdirectoru.com/articles/do-facilities-matter-recruiting/.

Jacobs, Peter. "Here's the Insane Amount of Time Student-Athletes Spend on Practice." *Business Insider*, January 27, 2015. https://www.businessinsider.com/college-student-athletes-spend-40-hours-a-week-practicing-2015-1.

Johnson, Richard. "College Football's Newest Coaches Have Some Interesting Incentives and Clauses in Their Contracts." *Sports Illustrated*, June 22, 2023. https://www.si.com/college/2023/06/22/coach-contracts-incentives-clauses.

Kelderman, Eric. "Who Should Oversee Athletes' Academic Progress?" *The Chronicle of Higher Education*, January 28, 2018. https://www.chronicle.com/article/who-should-oversee-athletes-academic-progress/.

Leroy, Michael H. "College Athletic Debt Soars as Power 5 Programs Resist Scrutiny." *Sportico*, January 5, 2022. https://www.sportico.com/leagues/college-sports/2022/college-athletic-debt-soars-1234651231/.

Litan, Robert E., Johnathan M. Orszag, and Peter R. Orszag. "The Empirical Effects of Collegiate Athletics: An Interim Report." Sebago Associates and The National Collegiate Athletic Association. 2003. https://ncaaorg

.s3.amazonaws.com/research/Finances/RES_EmpiricalEffectsOfCollegiate
AthleticsInterimReport.pdf

McCallum, Jack. "The Cruelest Thing Ever." *Sports Illustrated*, June 30, 1986.
https://vault.si.com/vault/1986/06/30/the-cruelest-thing-ever.

McMillen, Tom, and Paul Coggins. *Out of Bounds: How the American Sports
Establishment Is Being Driven by Greed and Hypocrisy—and What Needs to Be
Done about It.* New York: Simon and Schuster, 1992.

Memmott, Mark. "Report: Years and Years of Missed Chances in Penn State
Scandal." *NPR*, November 14, 2011. https://www.npr.org/sections/the
-two-way/2011/11/14/142298661/report-years-and-years-of-missed-chances
-in-penn-state-scandal.

Nakamura, David, and Mark Asher. "10 Years Later, Bias's Death Still Resonates."
Washington Post, June 19, 1996. https://www.washingtonpost.com/wp-srv
/sports/longterm/memories/bias/launch/bias19.htm.

NCAA. *Faculty Athletics Representative Handbook.* n.d. NCAA Faculty Athletics
Representative Association (FARA). Accessed February 15, 2024. https://
www.ncaafara.org/_files/ugd/ad7e32_ed76dc0c17884b4c9f5f8fa4144
7993b.pdf.

NCAA 2023–24 Division I Manual. NCAA. 2023. https://www.ncaapublications
.com/productdownloads/D124.pdf.

NCAA Eligibility Center Quick Reference Guide. NCAA Eligibility Center,
n.d. Accessed February 24, 2024. https://stanford_ftp.sidearmsports.com
/custompages/Compliance/InitialEligibilityQuickReferenceSheet.pdf.

"NCAA Graduation Rates: A Quarter-Century of Tracking Academic Success."
NCAA. October 28, 2014. https://www.ncaa.org/sports/2014/10/28
/ncaa-graduation-rates-a-quarter-century-of-tracking-academic-success
.aspx.

NCAA v. Board of Regents of University of Oklahoma, 468 U.S. 85 (1984). n.d.
Justia Law. Accessed February 15, 2024. https://supreme.justia.com/cases
/federal/us/468/85/.

NCSA College Recruiting. "NCAA Sliding Scale." https://www.ncsasports.org
/ncaa-eligibility-center/ncaa-sliding-scale. (April 192024).

New, Jake. "Attendance Monitoring Programs Common in College Athletics."
Inside Higher Ed, June 23, 2015. https://www.insidehighered.com/news
/2015/06/24/attendance-monitoring-programs-common-college-athletics.

New, Jake. "What CEOs Don't Know. Big-Time Colleges Were Rushing to Hire
Executives as Athletics Directors a Few Years Ago—but the Results Have
Some Questioning the Trend." *Inside Higher Ed*, November 6, 2014. https:

//www.insidehighered.com/news/2014/11/07/colleges-turn-athletics
-directors-business-background-results-vary#.

Olson, Eric. "Special Admissions Called 'Original Sin' of College Sports." *AP News*, March 16, 2019. https://apnews.com/article/a842ec11faa645b7 adf5e75034e8bbf4.

O'Neill, James M. "Rutgers Athletics Spends Big—and Builds Big Debt—to Stay Competitive in the Big Ten." *NorthJersey.com*. July 7, 2022. https://www.northjersey.com/story/news/watchdog/2022/07/07/rutgers -athletics-spends-big-builds-debt-big-ten-conference/65367819007/.

Porto, B., G. Gurney, D. Lopiano, D. B. Ridpath, A. Sack, M. Willingham, and A. Zimbalist. "The Drake Group Position Statement: Fixing the Dysfunctional NCAA Enforcement System." April 7, 2015. https://www .thedrakegroup.org/wp-content/uploads/2019/06/tdg-position-fair-ncaa -enforcement.pdf.

Quinn, Brendan F. "Johnny Orr (1926–2013), Who Built His Legacy at Michigan and Cemented It at Iowa State, Was More Than a Coach." *Mlive*. January 1, 2014. https://www.mlive.com/wolverines/2014/01/in_ remembrance_johnny_orr_1926.html.

"A Real Incentive or PR?" *Inside Higher Ed*, 2015. https://www.insidehighered .com/news/2015/02/06/academic-requirements-coaching-bonuses-rare.

"Restoring the Balance: Dollars, Values, and the Future of College Sports." Knight Commission on Intercollegiate Athletics. 2017. https://www.knightcommis sion.org/wp-content/uploads/2017/09/restoring-the-balance-0610-01.pdf.

Ridpath, B. David. *Alternative Models of Sports Development in America: Solutions to a Crisis in Education and Public Health on JSTOR*. 1st ed. Ohio University Press, 2018. https://doi.org/10.2307/j.ctv224twp0.

Ridpath, B. David. 2002. "NCAA Division I Student-Athlete Characteristics as Indicators of Academic Achievement and Graduation from College." PhD diss., West Virginia University. https://researchrepository.wvu.edu/etd/2428/.

Ridpath, B. David, Gerald Gurney, and Donna Lopiano. "Presidents Choose to Enable Academic Fraud in Athletics." *Journal of NCAA Compliance*, July–August 2019. https://journalncaacompliance.com/wp-content/uploads /2021/01/JONC-July-August-2019.pdf.

Ridpath, B. David, Gerald S. Gurney, and Eric M. Snyder. "NCAA Academic Fraud Cases and Historical Consistency: A Comparative Content Analysis." *Journal of the Legal Aspects of Sport* 25, no. 2 (2015): 75–103. https://doi .org/10.1123/jlas.2014-0021.

Ridpath, B. David, Mark Nagel, and Richard Southall. "New Rules for a New Ballgame: Legislative and Judicial Rationales for Revamping the NCAA's

Enforcement Process." *Entertainment and Sports Law Journal: Symposium Issue on College Sports and the Law* 6 (2008): 1.

Ridpath, D. B., B. Porto, G. Gurney, D. Lopiano, A. Sack, M. Willingham, and A. Zimbalist. "The Drake Group Position Statement: Student Fee Allocations to Fund Intercollegiate Athletics." The Drake Group. March 2, 2015. https://www.thedrakegroupeducationfund.org/wp-content/uploads/2019/06/position-statement-student-fees-final-3-2-15.pdf.

Rosenthal, Phil. "So Much for Chicago's Big Ten Team: 75 Years Ago, the University of Chicago Told the Conference It Wanted Out." *Chicago Tribune*, March 9, 2021. https://www.chicagotribune.com/2021/03/08/so-much-for-chicagos-big-ten-team-75-years-ago-the-university-of-chicago-told-the-conference-it-wanted-out/.

Ross v. Creighton University, 740 F. Supp. 1319 (N.D. Ill. 1990). 2001.

Sack, Allen, and Gerald Gurney. "The NCAA's Miraculous Graduation Rate! It Is Correct to Recognize Transfers Who Graduate, but the Flawed Formula Needs to Be Revisited." *Sports Business Journal*, May 6, 2019. https://www.sportsbusinessjournal.com/Journal/Issues/2019/05/06/Opinion/SackGurney.aspx.

Sailes, Gary A. "The Case against NCAA Proposition 48." In *African Americans in Sports*. New York: Routledge, 2017.

Salzwedel, Matthew R., and Jon Ericson. "Cleaning Up Buckley: How the Family Educational Rights and Privacy Act Shields Academic Corruption in College Athletics." *Wisconsin Law Review* (2003): 1053. https://heinonline.org/HOL/LandingPage?handle=hein.journals/wlr2003&div=41&id=&page=.

"Scandal as Big as All Texas: Cheating among the State's Football Recruiters Reaches Even to Governor's Mansion." *Los Angeles Times*, March 12, 2019. https://www.latimes.com/archives/la-xpm-1987-03-08-sp-13578-story.html.

Smith, Jay M., and Mary Willingham. *Cheated: The UNC Scandal, the Education of Athletes, and the Future of Big-Time College Sports*. University of Nebraska Press, 2019.

Splitt, Frank G. "The Student-Athlete: An NCAA False Claim?" The Drake Group Education Fund. 2019. https://www.thedrakegroupeducationfund.org/wp-content/uploads/2019/06/splitt_the_student_athlete.pdf.

Staurowsky, Ellen J., and B. David Ridpath. "The Case for Minimum 2.0 Standard for NCAA Division I Athletes." *Journal of Legal Aspects of Sport* 15 (2005): 113–38.

Steinbach, Paul. "Scholars React to Cancellation of NCAA Colloquium." *Athletic Business*, November 20, 2013. https://www.athleticbusiness.com/home/article/15142745/scholars-react-to-cancellation-of-ncaa-colloquium.

"Student-Athlete Opportunity Fund (SAOF)." George Washington University. Accessed February 15, 2024. https://gwsports.com/sports/2018/7/23/school-bio-student-athlete-opportunity-fund-html.

Student Right-to-Know and Campus Security Act, Pub. L. No. 101-542, 104 Stat. 2381 (1990).

Telander, Rick. "You Reap What You Sow." *Sports Illustrated*, February 27, 1989. https://vault.si.com/vault/1989/02/27/you-reap-what-you-sow-oklahoma-has-paid-the-price-for-the-anything-goes-attitude-that-coach-barry-switzer-has-allowed-to-take-root.

Thamel, Pete. "Top Grades and No Class Time for Auburn Players." *New York Times*, July 14, 2006. https://www.nytimes.com/2006/07/14/sports/ncaafootball/14auburn.html.

Thamel, Pete, and Duff Wilson. "Poor Grades Aside, Athletes Get into College on a \$399 Diploma." *New York Times*, November 27, 2005. https://www.nytimes.com/2005/11/27/sports/ncaafootball/poor-grades-aside-athletes-get-into-college-on-a-399.html.

Waller, Jeffrey M. "A Necessary Evil: Proposition 16 and Its Impact on Academics and Athletics in the NCAA." *DePaul Journal of Sports Law & Contemp. Problems* 1 (2003): 189–206.

Whitford, David. *A Payroll to Meet: A Story of Greed, Corruption, and Football at SMU*. New York: Macmillan, 1989.

Winters, Carla A., and Gerald S. Gurney. "Academic Preparation of Specially-Admitted Student-Athletes: A Question of Basic Skills." *College and University* 88, no. 2 (2012): 2–9.

Wolverton, Brad. "College Football Players Spend 44.8 Hours a Week on Their Sport, NCAA Survey Finds." *The Chronicle of Higher Education*, January 14, 2008. https://www.chronicle.com/article/college-football-players-spend-44-8-hours-a-week-on-their-sport-ncaa-survey-finds-395/.

Wolverton, Brad. "Spending Plenty So Athletes Can Make the Grade." *The Chronicle of Higher Education*, September 5, 2008. https://www.chronicle.com/article/spending-plenty-so-athletes-can-make-the-grade/.

Zimbalist, Andrew. "Sports Hiatus Gives NCAA an Opportunity to Rethink the Structure of College Sports." *Forbes*, April 25, 2020. https://www.forbes.com/sites/andrewzimbalist/2020/04/25/sports-being-on-hiatus-gives-ncaa-an-opportunity-to-rethink-the-structure-of-college-sports/?sh=2dd34e4c3h54

AUTHOR'S WORKS

Gurney, Gerald S. "Pickpockets at the Gallows: SMU's Death Penalty and Today's Recruiting Meat Market." *Sportico*, January 18, 2022. https://www.sportico .com/leagues/college-sports/2022/smu-death-penalty-echoes-1234658415/.

Gurney, Gerald, Lisa Rubin, Sarah Stokowski, and B. David Ridpath. "The Original Sin of College Sports: College Presidents' Ineffectual Use of Special Admissions." *Journal of NCAA Compliance*, 2020. https://tigerprints.clemson .edu/cgi/viewcontent.cgi?article=1017&context=ed_org_ldrshp_pub.

Ridpath, B. David, and Gerald Gurney. "Opinion: After a Decade of Mark Emmert, NCAA Needs New Leadership." *Oklahoman*, July 5, 2020. https:// www.oklahoman.com/story/sports/columns/berry-tramel/2020/07/05/gur ney-says-mark-emmerts-time-is-passed-as-ncaa-president/60393253007/.

Gurney, Gerald, Ramogi Huma, Ellen Staurowsky, and Mary Willingham. "How Colleges Cheat Student-Athletes." Senate panel hosted by Senator Chris Murphy. Washington, DC, July 25, 2019. https://www.facebook.com /senchrismurphy/videos/480132192387869?s=1027693677&v=e&sfns=mo.

Ridpath, B. David, Gerald Gurney, and Donna Lopiano. "Presidents Choose to Enable Academic Fraud in Athletics." *Journal of NCAA Compliance*, July– August 2019, 3–6. https://journalncaacompliance.com/wp-content/uploads /2021/01/JONC-July-August-2019.pdf.

Gurney, Gerald S. "How to (Maybe) Reduce Academic Fraud in Athletics." *The Chronicle of Higher Education*, January 28, 2018. https://www.chronicle.com /article/how-to-maybe-reduce-academic-fraud-in-athletics/.

Gurney, Gerald. "Transfer Restrictions on Football and Athlete Freedom." In *College Athletes' Rights and Well-Being: Critical Perspectives on Policy and Practice*, ed. Eddie Comeaux. JHU Press, 2017.

Gurney, Gerald, Woodrow Eckard, and Richard Southall. "The Hoax of NCAA Graduation Rates." *Sports Litigation Alert*, 2017. https://sportslitigationalert .com/the-hoax-of-ncaa-graduation-rates/.

Gurney, Gerald, Donna Lopiano, and Andrew Zimbalist. 2017. *Unwinding Madness: What Went Wrong with College Sports and How to Fix It*. Washington, DC: Brookings Institute, 2017.

Gurney, Gerald, and Donna Lopiano. "The College Sports Wasteland." *Modern Sports Ethics: A Reference Handbook*, ed. Angela Lumpkin. 2nd ed. Bloomsbury, 2016.

Sack, Allen, and Gerald Gurney. "Excessive and Exploitive Demands." *Inside Higher Ed*, March 22, 2016. https://www.insidehighered.com/views/2016/03/22/college-athletes-must-spend-unreasonable-amount-time-their-sports-essay.

Gurney, Gerald S., and B. David Ridpath. "Why the NCAA Continues to Work against Athletes' Best Interests." *The Chronicle of Higher Education*, February 29, 2016. https://www.chronicle.com/article/why-the-ncaa-continues-to-work-against-athletes-best-interests/.

Gurney, G., E. Lopiano, D. Snyder, M. Willingham, J. Meyer, B. Porto, D. B. Ridpath, A. Sack, and A. Zimbalist. "The Drake Group Education Fund Position Statement: Why the NCAA Academic Progress Rate (APR) and Graduation Success Rate (GSR) Should Be Abandoned and Replaced with More Effective Academic Metrics." The Drake Group Education Fund. 2015. https://thedrakegroupeducationfund.org/2015/06/07/drake-group-questions-ncaa-academic-metrics/.

Ridpath, B. David, Gerald S. Gurney, and Eric M. Snyder. "NCAA Academic Fraud Cases and Historical Consistency: A Comparative Content Analysis." *Journal of the Legal Aspects of Sport* 25, no. 2 (2015): 75–103. https://doi.org/10.1123/jlas.2014-0021.

Ridpath, D. B., B. Porto, G. Gurney, D. Lopiano, A. Sack, M. Willingham, and A. Zimbalist. "The Drake Group Position Statement: Student Fee Allocations to Fund Intercollegiate Athletics." The Drake Group. March 2, 2015. https://www.thedrakegroupeducationfund.org/wp-content/uploads/2019/06/position-statement-student-fees-final-3-2-15.pdf.

Porto, B., G. Gurney, D. Lopiano, D. B. Ridpath, A. Sack, M. Willingham, A. Zimbalist. "The Drake Group Position Statement: Fixing the Dysfunctional NCAA Enforcement System." The Drake Group. April 7, 2015. https://www.thedrakegroup.org/wp-content/uploads/2019/06/tdg-position-fair-ncaa-enforcement.pdf.

Gurney, Gerald. Interview. *The Bob Edwards Show*. "Dropping the Ball: The Shady Side of Big-Time College Sports." Sirius XM Satellite Radio, September 22, 2014.

Gurney, Gerald. Interview. *Real Sports with Bryant Gumbel*. Season 20, episode 3, "Gaming the System." HBO, March 25, 2014.

Gurney, Gerald, and Mary Willingham. 2014. "Academic Fraud, Athletes and Faculty Responsibility." *Inside Higher Ed*, July 17, 2014. https://www

.insidehighered.com/views/2014/07/18/professors-must-take-academic -fraud-among-athletes-more-seriously-essay.

Porto, Brian, Gerald Gurney, Donna A. Lopiano, B. David Ridpath, Allen Sack, Mary Willingham, and Andrew Zimbalist. "The 'Big Five' Power Grab: The Real Threat to College Sports." *The Chronicle of Higher Education*, June 19, 2014. https://www.chronicle.com/article/the-big-five-power-grab-the -real-threat-to-college-sports/.

Gurney, Gerald, and Richard M. Southall. "NCAA Reform Gone Wrong." *Inside Higher Ed*, February 13, 2013. https://www.insidehighered.com /views/2013/02/14/ncaa-academic-reform-has-hurt-higher-eds-integrity -essay.

Gurney, Gerald S., and Richard M. Southall. 2012. "College Sports' Bait and Switch." *ESPN*, August 9, 2012. https://www.espn.com/college-sports/story/ _/id/8248046/college-sports-programs-find-multitude-ways-game-ncaa-apr.

Winters, Carla A., and Gerald S. Gurney. "Academic Preparation of Specially-Admitted Student-Athletes: A Question of Basic Skills." *College and University* 88, no. 2 (2012): 2–9.

Dennie, Christian S., and Gerald S. Gurney. "It's Time for the NCAA to Get It Right." *The Chronicle of Higher Education*, January 8, 2012. https://www .chronicle.com/article/its-time-for-the-ncaa-to-get-it-right/.

Gurney, Gerald S. "Stop Lowering the Bar for College Athletes." *The Chronicle of Higher Education*, April 10, 2011. https://www.chronicle.com/article /stop-lowering-the-bar-for-college-athletes/.

Gurney, Gerald S. "Toughen NCAA Standards for Freshmen." *Inside Higher Ed*, February 6, 2011. https://www.insidehighered.com/views/2011/02/07 /toughen-ncaa-standards-freshmen.

Gurney, Gerald S., David Tan, and Carla Winters. "Specially Admitted Student-Athletes: Their Academic Performance, Persistence, and Graduation from an NCAA Football Bowl Subdivision University." *International Journal of Sport Management* 11, no. 3 (2010): 477–91.

Gurney, Gerald S. "Now We Must Reform Athletics Reform." *The Chronicle of Higher Education*, October 18, 2009. https://www.chronicle.com/article /now-we-must-reform-athletics-reform/.

Gurney, Gerald S., and Jerome C. Weber. "The Coaches' Graduation Rate: A Catalyst for Academically Responsible Behavior." *College and University* 84, no. 2 (2008): 53.

Gurney, Gerald S., and Jerome C. Weber. "A Better Way to Measure Coaches' Wins and Losses." *The Chronicle of Higher Education*, October 24, 2008. https://www.chronicle.com/article/a-better-way-to-measure-coaches-wins -and-losses/.

Gurney, Gerald S., and Jerome C. Weber. "Rethinking the NCAA's Academic Reform." *College and University* 83, no. 2 (2007): 47.

Gurney, Gerald S., and Jerome C. Weber. "Professors Must Speak Out: Colleges Can No Longer Afford Athletics as Usual." *The Chronicle of Higher Education*, April 5, 2010. https://www.chronicle.com/article/professors-must-speak-out-colleges-can-no-longer-afford-athletics-as-usual/.

Gurney, Gerald S., and Debra L. Stuart. "Effects of Special Admission, Varsity Competition, and Sports on Freshman Student-Athletes' Academic Performance." *Journal of College Student Personnel*, 1987.

Gurney, Gerald S. Editorial. *Academic Athletic Journal* 1 (spring 1986). https://hdl.handle.net/2097/43172.

Gurney, Gerald S., and Sally P. Johnston. 1986. "Advising the Student-Athlete." *Academic Athletic Journal* 1 (spring 1986): 35–38. https://hdl.handle.net/2097/43178.

Mathes, S., and G. Gurney. "Factors in Student Athlete's Choice of Colleges." *Journal of College Student Personnel* 26, no. 4 (July 1985).

Gurney, G., D. Robinson, and L. Fygetakis. "Athletic Academic Counseling within NCAA Institutions: A National Profile of Staff, Training, and Services." *Athletic Administration* 17, no. 3 (spring 1983).

Gurney, Gerald, and Daniel Robinson. "The Student Athlete: An Institutional Responsibility—A Model for Academic Athletic Support." *The National Advisor*, fall 1981.

ABOUT THE AUTHOR AND CONTRIBUTORS

Gerald S. Gurney, PhD, (1951–2022) retired in 2022 as professor emeritus of Academic Affairs at the University of Oklahoma, where he served as senior associate athletic director for Academics and Student Life from 1993 to 2011. Previously, Dr. Gurney held positions as associate athletic director for academic support and compliance at the University of Maryland, College Park; assistant athletic director for academic affairs at Southern Methodist University; athletic academic counselor at Iowa State University; and academic adviser at Grinnell College. His professional expertise encompassed critical issues in intercollegiate athletics, including the impact on higher education, academic support, reform, and ethics. Dr. Gurney authored or coauthored approximately forty publications—including *Unwinding Madness: What Went Wrong with College Sports and How to Fix It*—and delivered more than thirty major presentations, including a US Senate panel on academic integrity in college sports in 2019. He appeared in documentaries such as *Schooled: The Price of College Sports* (EPIX), *Gaming the System* (HBO), and *Dropping the Ball: The Shady Side of Big-Time College Sports* (SiriusXM and NPR). Dr. Gurney received numerous awards, including honors from The Drake Group (TDG), National Association of Academic and Student-Athlete Development (N4A) (the Lan Hewlett Award—N4A's highest honor), Japan Association for College and University Education, Oklahoma Psychological Association, University of Oklahoma Department of Educational Leadership and Policy Studies, and Oklahoma County Mental Health Association. Dr. Gurney served as president of the National Association of Academic Advisers for Athletics (N4A) from 2010 to 2011 and president of TDG from 2014 to 2016. Throughout his career, Dr. Gurney worked directly with well-known celebrity coaches (e.g., Bob Stoops, Mack Brown, Mike Leach, Bobby Collins, Mark Mangino, Kevin Sumlin, Johnny Orr, and Kelvin Sampson). He also worked directly with thousands of athletes such as Heisman winners Sam Bradford and Jason White, and many other great athletes (e.g., Blake Griffin, Adrian Peterson, and Josh Heupel).

Visit www.geraldgurney.com to learn more about Dr. Gurney, his many works, and the University of Oklahoma Dr. Gerald S. Gurney Retention Scholarship Fund.

Donna A. Lopiano, PhD, is the president of Sports Management Resources, a consulting firm that assists colleges and universities in athletics program strategic planning, gender equity, and growth and development challenges. She is also an adjunct professor of sports management at Southern Connecticut State University; past president of

TDG, an academic think tank working on reform of college athletics; and a member of the Women's Sports Policy Working Group, tackling issues related to the participation of trans girls and women in girls' and women's sports. Dr. Lopiano formerly served as the University of Texas at Austin Director of Women's Athletics and CEO of the Women's Sports Foundation. She is coauthor of the *Athletic Director's Desk Reference* with Connee Zotos and *Unwinding Madness: What Went Wrong with College Sports and How to Fix It* with Gerald Gurney and Andrew Zimbalist.

Dr. B. David Ridpath, EdD, is finishing his second decade as a tenured faculty member with Ohio University and its prestigious Sports Administration Program as a professor of sports business. He is also a member at-large with the Ohio University Faculty Alliance (AAUP) and is involved in its current faculty unionization effort. Prior to Ohio University, he was an assistant professor of sport administration at Mississippi State University and has more than fifteen years of practical experience in intercollegiate athletics in administrative and coaching capacities at Marshall University, Weber State University, and Ohio University. Dr. Ridpath is often cited by major worldwide media outlets such as the *New York Times*, *Time* magazine, CNN, and ESPN as an expert on NCAA and intercollegiate athletic matters due to his research and practical experience in the industry. Dr. Ridpath has appeared before congressional committees and has served as an expert witness in numerous cases involving intercollegiate athletics and college athlete rights. An accomplished researcher, he has authored more than thirty academic journal articles, ten academic book chapters and monographs, and two books. His latest book is *Alternative Models of Sport Development in America: Solutions to a Crisis in Education and Public Health*.

Mary Willingham has served as a teacher and literacy director for KIPP Public Schools, faculty adjunct at Durham Technical Community College, learning specialist and assistant director for the Center for Student Success and Academic Counseling, and clinical instructor in the School of Education at the University of North Carolina, Chapel Hill.

Willingham's research and writing focus on the NCAA and university admission procedures with regard to athletes and their specific gaps in basic skill deficits, as well as the incidence of learning disabilities and attention deficit hyperactivity disorder. She is the co-author of *Cheated: The UNC Scandal, the Education of Athletes, and the Future of Big-Time College Sports*, about the academic and athletic fraud case at UNC. Its publication led to several media appearances including three documentaries, a TEDx Talk, as well as ongoing litigation and congressional testimonies supporting athletes' rights to a real education. The University of South Carolina Library archives a collection of Willingham's writings and supporting documentation.